DARE TO SUCCEED

DARE TO SUCCEED

How to Survive and Thrive in the Game of Life

MARK BURNETT

HYPERION NEW YORK

ISBN 0-7868-6849-X

FIRST EDITION
10 9 8 7 6 5 4 3 2 1

To those who want to go . . .
above, beyond and then further.

Acknowledgments

There are so many people who contributed to my real-life "daring to succeed" that it would be impossible to list them all. Instead I think I will confine my acknowledgments to those directly involved in the writing of this book, those who have worked with me since the beginning, and those who gave me the breaks.

Firstly, Marty Dugard, with whom I worked on my previous two books, again played an enormous role in guiding me through this process. He is an incredible author in his own right and loves adventure. I hope we work together again for many years to come. Other huge contributors were Mary Ellen O'Neill at Hyperion and my awesome personal staff of Spencer Rosenberg, Chris Wilkas, Diane Winkler, and Rachael Harrell. And the book deal would never have been made without the hard work of Scott Waxman and Conrad Riggs.

As mentioned in the book, my current core Eco-Challenge management team, who have been there since the beginning and are at the center of my success, are Lisa Hennessy, Amanda Harrell, and Tricia Middleton. Also, Brian Terkelsen was the very first member of my "Eco" management team and always shared my "Eco" vision. Thanks, guys. There are of course many more *Eco-Challenge* and *Survivor* producers, editors, associate producers, assistant editors, accountants, and production assistants. It's a big, talented team numbering in the hundreds and you know who you are.

There were a number of people who gave me my pivotal TV breaks. They are, in order: Don Meek, Beth Maharry, Gerard Supeau, Doug Herzog, Greg Moyer, Leslie Moonves, Ghen Maynard, Gordon Beck, Stephen Chao, Garth Ancier, and Scott Sassa. Again, Conrad Riggs played a huge role in most of this.

Clearly, I owe a huge thanks to my family for making me believe I could do anything I wanted, and who have continually put up with my fairly long absences caused by my fairly selfish adventures. I also owe a lot to the Parachute Regiment for making me understand the value of tenacity and adventure.

DARE TO SUCCEED

The American Dream

Ever since I was a child, I've cherished the American Dream. The term is broad, and has been invoked for a variety of reasons by everyone from presidents to Madison Avenue, perhaps diluting its meaning along the way. So I think a definition is in order. To me, the American Dream means anything is possible. Any individual willing to work hard, develop their natural talents, and persevere when the going gets tough can see their goals realized. No other place on earth offers such an opportunity as the United States of America.

I should know. The American Dream has come to define my life.

The moment, however, when I felt the power of the American Dream more than any other occurred on Memorial Day, 2000. My family and I were in Malibu, celebrating at the home of a treasured friend. Burt is an extremely successful man, and his beach house sprawls across four oceanfront lots. As we chatted while drinking Chardonnay on the deck, it struck me that the setting couldn't have been more idyllic: Before me on the sand, my two young sons played near the Pacific. The sky was a cloudless blue. And the combination of salty soft breeze and dry white wine lent a distinctly Californian touch that was a far cry from my childhood in London's gray and grimy East End.

Yet, at a time when I should have been relaxing, I felt restless, in need of reassurance. In just three days my first network television show, *Survivor*, would premier on CBS. I'd labored years for that day, withstanding obstacles and rejection because my gut told me *Survivor* was destined to be a hit. CBS shared my intuition. They had worked hard promoting the show, coming up with dozens of ingenious publicity stunts. I never knew when another would pop up out of the blue to remind me that this pet project I'd nurtured for so long was being thrown into the oft-fickle den of American public opinion. My nagging need for reassurance came from worries that this pivotal, long-awaited moment in my career might, despite what my gut said, turn out to be a failure.

I swatted the negative ruminations aside. I'd come so far, I reminded myself. I'd taken enormous chances, embraced risk, and refused to blink when failure stared me down. I was a poster child for the American Dream, and my presence at Burt's home was ironic evidence of that. He was the man who gave me one of my first jobs when I came to America in 1982. The occupation had nothing to do with adventure or television or even sales-manship, the three hallmarks of my career. When I worked for Burt I was nanny to his two children. My salary was $250 per week. In addition to baby-sitting, my duties included helping with homework, running er-rands, driving two boys to and from school, and coach-ing basketball (this, by a man who'd never so much as dribbled a ball before coming to America). Now almost two decades later I was not only a regularly invited guest in that very same house, but producer of the most an-ticipated summer television show in history. I'd come a long way.

I came to America fresh off a stint in the British Para-troopers. I was a naïve young ex-soldier with just $600 cash in my pocket and a deep fear of failure. I had no advanced formal education. No family wealth to fall back on. No business connections. No marketable skills. I was flying to America to make something of myself. But I had long idealized the American Dream. My gut told me that I could do anything I wanted in America. All I had to do was work my ass off.

Well, it turned out it takes a lot more than that. I learned that success certainly requires hard work, but it's also about passion, knowledge, self-awareness, and ample doses of courage. For instance, beyond having Burt as a mentor, many extremely successful people were houseguests at Burt's. Successful people enjoy talk-ing about their success, especially to people genuinely interested in learning from their experience. I learned the ways of the business world by continually asking them question after question about how they got to where they were, what mistakes they made along the way, and how they conducted their businesses. Was I nervous asking them? Sure. But I had nothing to lose, and everything to gain (remember, I was a nanny). The worst thing that could happen was that they would refuse to talk with me. When that happened, I brushed aside the rejection, mustered up my courage once again, and waited for the next houseguest.

One of the nicest and most encouraging was Burt's friend, a young movie producer named Sherry Lansing. Her advice was to return every call every day, listen to all ideas, never be condescending, and above all to believe in myself. She believed that being nice and being successful were not mutually exclusive. It paid off for her. She's now head of Paramount Pictures.

I used these and many other early insights to climb a most improbable ladder of success: from soldier to nanny to T-shirt salesman to professional adventurer to television producer, learning the art of focus along the way. I learned to look at business problems from every angle, sometimes deciding that the best plan of attack was the one that appeared silly or downright stupid. My tactics were unusual, but they generally worked. When they didn't, I learned from the mistake and tried again. I never (with the exception of one very educational incident) quit. I refused to accept the word *no* and eventually decided I would not even hear it anymore. I formulated a set of seven principles that govern how I run my life: 1. Only results count; 2. Have the courage to fail; 3. Choose teammates wisely; 4. Perseverance produces character; 5. Be right or be wrong, but make a decision; 6. Set achievable goals; and, 7. Try to go above, beyond, and then further.

No formula exists that will guarantee success. But those seven principles guided me through the minefield dividing dreams and success. I wouldn't be where I am today without them. They're simple, they're intense, and they work.

I first heard the idea that was to become *Survivor* in 1995, while at Fox television in Los Angeles pitching *Eco-Challenge*. Lauren Correo, the exec hearing the *Eco* pitch, told me about this game show concept where a bunch of people starved on a desert island. They competed for luxuries such as food and pillows. Meanwhile, a host living a sultan's existence on a luxury yacht offshore eliminates them from the contest, one by one.

The brains behind this game show concept was Charlie Parsons, a prolific British producer. Lauren loved the idea, but believed it would take someone with previous experience producing large-scale adventure-reality TV in a remote setting to pull it off. *Eco-Challenge* (in her mind) qualified me. In the days and months after that meeting, I constantly thought about the island game show, though I saw it more as a drama. When I traveled for business I would look about the plane at my fellow passengers and imagine us crash-landing on an island.

Where would I fit into our new society? Who would lead? Who would follow? Who would find the ordeal too hard and quit?

I made it my goal to meet Charlie and show him *Eco-Challenge*. We hit it off and I ended up buying the North American rights to his island show in 1998. I had a gut feeling that I could make this great concept even greater. My *Survivor* would be bigger, more dramatic, and more epic than any non-fiction television ever seen.

But first I had to convince a network to pay the production costs, which would run into millions of dollars. I began practicing my sales pitch. I would only get one chance to pitch it to a network or cable channel, and didn't want to blow it. My practice consisted of pitching friends and acquaintances at dinner parties. Not that I told them they were guinea pigs. Simply, at some time during dinner, someone would invariably ask what I was working on next. I would smile, take a deep breath, raise my voice just a notch for greater emphasis, then explain *Survivor* as brilliantly and boldly and seductively as I possibly could.

When I was still trying to figure out the pitch, it often came out as long-winded and over-complicated. My dinner companions would lean back in their chairs, heads nodding vacantly as if listening, even as their eyes glazed over and their thoughts wandered. They would hear me out, but then the conversation would diplomatically shift to another topic.

As I perfected the pitch, however, making it faster

and fluid and always exciting, I began to notice my dinner companions leaning in to hear each syllable. Their eyes sparkled. They peppered me with follow-up questions, all of which I learned to answer with the same polish as the pitch itself. By the time I walked into Discovery Channel's headquarters in 1999 to pitch the show for the first time for real, I was capable of selling it to anyone, anywhere.

Or so I thought. Mike Quattrone at Discovery turned me down flat. He said it wasn't right for their brand. I was stunned. Discovery had been my partner on *Eco-Challenge* since 1996. We had a solid working relationship and they were the natural place for a show about adventure, nature, and drama. Mentally, I'd counted on them buying the show. I was devastated.

But, as is my modus operandi—moving forward, always forward—I pitched *Survivor* everywhere it seemed appropriate—and was rejected at every turn, including by USA Network (where Steve Chao turned it down in less than thirty seconds, then announced out of left field that he wanted to buy *Eco-Challenge*) and Fox (where David Hill said I should first produce and televise it in Australia to see if it worked. He warned that if I messed up my first network show in the United States it would be my last). By the way, Steve and David are now friends of mine and are both brilliant TV minds who are highly unusual in their willingness to laugh publicly at their *Survivor* passes—something less confident execs would never admit.

The passes continued: NBC, then ABC, and finally CBS. Yes, CBS passed!! Tom Noonan, president at UPN, loved the concept, but the fledging network couldn't offer enough money for me to put together a quality production. Although I was tempted, I knew exactly how I wanted *Survivor* to look and feel, and that I needed a sufficient budget. Knowing it was for the best, I mustered up my courage and turned UPN down.

Then, unbelievably, I got another chance to pitch CBS. This time it was Ghen Maynard in their Drama division. Ghen immediately liked what he heard and took the idea to CBS President Leslie Moonves, who was intrigued by *Survivor,* but wanted to hear me pitch it in person. I should have been nervous going in to see one of the legendary tough guys of network TV, but I have never been more calm. Confidently, my skills polished at all those dinner parties and previous pitches, I walked into Leslie's enormous office and delivered the pitch of my life. I added during this pitch that I was certain I could help CBS pack the advertising into sponsorship packages similar to large sporting events. He bought the show, approving a large-enough budget under the condition that I help line up advertisers before filming began. He wanted to see if the advertising community would embrace this novel program, and whether I could deliver on my sponsorship concept.

The moment Leslie said yes was one of the most exciting and horrifying of my life. Exciting, because I was finally in the big leagues. I'd sold a television show to one of America's big three networks. Anyone in America with a television could watch. Cable wasn't a prerequisite. The potential audience was massive, which was enormously frightening.

Survivor would mean a nationwide contestant search followed by thirty-nine days of filming in the South China Sea. The logistics were incredible. Was I good enough to pull it off? Would America embrace my quirky little show or would they laugh at my surreal Tribal Councils, native "art direction," and overly serious confessionals? Beyond my dramatic intentions, what if someone died? And what about the promise of helping to sell commercial minutes before production began? Had I been crazy to make such a promise?

That's when I took a deep breath, quieted the doubts, and remembered I needed to believe in myself. The show would work. I had always surrounded myself with good people. I had made quality adventure-reality television for five years. Plus, I had always played a huge role in securing advertisers for *Eco-Challenge* on Discovery Channel. I knew my stuff. As long as everyone did their jobs and I did mine, *Survivor* would turn out fantastic.

I got to work immediately, sending location scouts around the world to find the ideal *Survivor* island. Next I attacked the financial issue. I worked with CBS Advertising Sales to design sponsorships instead of merely commercial time, offering advertisers on-air product placement if they put their money behind *Survivor*. The sponsorship product-placement concept was relatively new for a network television series, though I had been doing it for years as a necessity for *Eco-Challenge.* I learned it through studying the financial sponsorship model for the Olympics. I was positive the sponsorship model would work with *Survivor,* too—and it did. Advertisers embraced the new show. Every sponsorship was sold before we began filming. *Survivor* was already a financial success. All we had to do was get the same number of viewers that CBS ordinarily would get from summer reruns. I knew we could do that.

Of course, I still wanted to get huge ratings. I pride myself on crafting absorbing television. Earning the money is fine, but at the end of the day, my biggest rush comes from overhearing people honestly rave about something I've produced.

The filming of *Survivor* was one challenge after another. Nothing I'd filmed for *Eco*—not the sandstorms of Morocco, not the cyclones off the Great Barrier Reef, not the blizzards of Patagonia—compared with the travails of Pulau Tiga. From the tempestuous equatorial weather to the sea snakes to the daily spectacle of Richard's nudity, there was never a dull moment. And the excitement didn't end when we flew back to civilization. The five short weeks between the end of location filming and Memorial Day weekend were a whirlwind of editing, publicity, high-level secrecy, and meeting after meeting after meeting with CBS to make sure the show had the perfect tone for their audience demographic.

The first show was now "locked" ("finished" in TV talk) but to say I was feeling edgy as I drove the two minutes from my home to Burt's on Memorial Day was an understatement. Even I, who always decided not to stress out about that which I couldn't control, simply could not put up with the idea of America disliking my show.

In hindsight, those fears were unfounded. *Survivor's* astronomical success now seems like a given. But before the show aired—before America met Pulau Tiga and the sixteen original castaways, and before Jeff Probst made "the tribe has spoken" part of the national vernacular—there were no guarantees that anyone would tune in for thirteen consecutive weeks. Television history is full of new shows bursting onto the screen full of hope then slinking off to anonymity a few weeks later.

By the time Burt and I sat down on his deck, I'd calmed down a bit. I was still hoping for that reassuring omen, but otherwise the only remnant of my rumination was that American Dream loop playing over and over in my head. I became aware that those seven guiding principles of mine had been proven correct again and again through six years of *Eco-Challenge* and in getting *Survivor* to its network premier. I felt more than a little awed that I'd gone from servant to holiday guest.

As if reading my thoughts, Burt pointed to the sprawling beachfront home next door. It was a single-lot teardown, but the view and location meant it was selling for 3.7 million dollars. "That house is for sale," Burt said. "Whoopi Goldberg was over looking at it the other day."

Jokingly, I said, "I should make an offer and buy that house. That would be the epitome of the American dream. From rags to riches. Everything would come full circle."

"No. You got it all wrong. You should buy *this* house and *I'd* buy that house," Burt corrected. "You'd be living on the big property while I move into the small place next door—*that* would be the American dream coming full circle."

We laughed. He was right, of course. Left unsaid was that my American Dream was still very much a work in progress. *Survivor* would be just the beginning. Through courage, naiveté, and hustle, I'd achieved a number of outstanding results, built a little wealth, lived in nice home just off the beach, and climbed onto the ladder of success. But I was still many rungs below living on the same beach as the most influential movers and shakers in the entertainment industry. Maybe someday, *Survivor* would take me there.

That's when a most outrageous thing occurred. The legendary screenwriter William Goldman has written of what he calls "movie moments"—real-life coincidences so stunning and pivotal they normally occur only on the silver screen. That Memorial Day, sipping Chardonnay with Burt, I experienced a movie moment. It literally flashed across the sky. For as we sat there, an airplane towing an advertisement banner flew along the beach, just a hundred feet above the ocean. I ignored it at first—such airplanes are common in Southern California, especially on holiday weekends. But when I finally read the banner I was shocked: It promoted my *Survivor* premier in three days' time. Burt and I gazed at it in disbelief. I felt more than a little proud that my old boss from my servant days truly understood the significance of how far I'd come.

If that had happened in a movie, the audience would immediately recognize the banner as foreshadowing of great things to come. That's how I chose to approach it in real life. I had come to America with nothing, and now the fruits of my labors were being touted in the skies above Malibu. The airplane was the reassurance I needed. *Survivor* was destined to become a hit. My American Dream, I knew, was destined to come true.

And you know what? Because of my seven principles, it has.

Only Results Count

MY OWN PATH TO SUCCESS began on my flight to America in October, 1982. In those eleven hours between London and Los Angeles, I discovered the importance of flexible strategizing. When the inevitable roadblock stops forward progress, take a moment, think, and find a clever way around it. Banging against a roadblock again and again simply leads to frustration and inertia.

When I first decided to leave England for America, I thought success would be obtained by using my military skills. My intention was to stop in Los Angeles, then fly down to Central America where I had heard a former SAS (Special Air Service—Britain's equivalent of the Green Berets) operative could offer someone like me a good living as a "military adviser." Central America was a hotbed of intrigue and power ploys at the time. I wasn't told the name of the country where I would be working, but the rumor mill of my elite military unit spoke of salaries in excess of $1000 per week. I would be training Latin military forces. The pay was a fortune compared with what I received as section commander in the British Army Parachute Regiment. I believed that working as a military adviser would help me set some money aside, smooth my transition into civilian life, then move on to some other occupation, which would lead me—hopefully—to success. I was 22 and naïve to the ways of the world (I didn't even know that Hollywood was in the same state as Los Angeles, let alone right next door). As strategies for success went, starting as a military adviser seemed to make sense.

An unlikely roadblock presented itself in the form of my mother. She was a factory worker, laboring in the battery compound next to the Ford Motors plant where my father worked. She always dressed immaculately, never letting her station in life interfere with how she presented herself. Not wanting her to be scared about what I would be doing, I had told her of a "security job" waiting for me in Los Angeles. She accepted the explanation without question. But when we were saying good-bye at Heathrow, she admitted to misgivings. "I've got a bad feeling about that security job in Los Angeles," she told me. "Maybe you should think it over before accepting it."

My mother's intuition had influenced her for as long as I could remember. The interesting thing is that she never voiced such a concern during any of my previous years in the Parachute Regiment—a stint that included dangerous duty in Northern Ireland and combat in the Falkland Islands War. She always "knew" I'd be okay.

The scene at Heathrow mirrored my mother's discomforting words. That airport is the crossroads of the aviation world, and people from all nationalities surged around us, running to planes, saying farewell to loved ones, or just looking jet-lagged after a transoceanic journey. My father was taking the train in from London to meet us at the departure gate, but had been delayed. So not only might I miss the chance to say farewell to my father, but I might have to leave my beloved mother tearful and alone in the harried terminal when I caught my plane. The mental picture of her standing alone, hoping to find my father in that enormous jumble of terminals, tore me apart. But her own comfort was the least of her worries. She was more concerned about me. Wiping away her tears, my mother looked me directly in the eyes and asked me to reconsider my future.

I was an only child, showered with unconditional love. While I was in the Army, my working-class mother had cashed in her retirement fund to surprise me with a new MG Roadster! My mother had also never unfairly criticized my aspirations. In fact, she had encouraged me by telling me that although we were poor and she couldn't afford to give me an expensive education, I could achieve anything I wanted. She used to tell me the story of the owner of the Woolworth's chain of stores who had started by selling from a shopping cart in London's East End (I never checked to see if the story was true, but it made me believe anything was possible). Basically, she had supported every crazy thing I had ever done my whole life, so I knew that what she was telling me came from a genuinely fearful intuition instead of a desire to see me remain in England or compromise my dreams. I had inherited her deep trust in intuition (or "going with my gut," as I like to say), and secretly also felt concern about going to Central America. But I was so eager to come to the United States and chase the American Dream I'd idealized since childhood that I ignored my nagging inner voice. That voice has never once failed me—as long as I heeded it. We've all got that little voice inside of us. It's sometimes scary to follow this voice, but I believe you get in more trouble by not listening to it.

I told my mother I would reconsider the security job. She knew I would. I would never, ever lie to my mother.

On the entire flight to America I pondered my future. I pondered not just the sanity of taking a job in Central America, but the outcome of my life. What outcome did I want? To be a big success. What was my more immediate goal? To find a job and a place to live. By the time I landed and cleared customs, I'd made up my mind: My military days were over. I would stay in Los Angeles and make a new life. My fear of failure would prove the catalyst. I couldn't imagine returning home to East London as anything less than a total success.

In many ways, changing strategies was more of a risk

than continuing on to Central America. At least there my military skills would be somewhat marketable. Short of becoming a felon, my knowledge of weapons, explosives, and tactics had no place in the Greater Los Angeles metropolitan area.

But I was always comfortable with risk—probably more so than with the easy life. My astrological sign is Cancer, the crab, which is often synonymous with tenacity and never letting go. Mere tenacity can overcome enormous odds. When combined with a healthy fear of failure, goals can be achieved instead of dropped by the wayside. Dreams are realized. Failure is never fatal, merely a setback. Tenacity empowers me to do anything (within moral and ethical limits) to succeed. I knew that tenacity, combined with my desire to succeed, would eventually get me where I wanted in America.

As luck would have it, my friend Nick had arranged to pick me up at the airport. He knew nothing of my Central American connection, just that I needed a place to stay for a few days. Therefore, he needed no explanation for my changing plans. He, too, had come from England, and had gotten a job as a chauffeur. He liked the work, and got to drive around in a Lamborghini. Nick even took advantage of his boss's business travels to act like he owned his boss' car and house.

As we drove from the airport to Nick's apartment, I was amazed at my first glimpse of America, with its giant billboards, huge cars, and 12-lane freeways. Everything was bigger than back home. I even saw my first drive-thru fast food restaurant on that drive. I never knew such a thing existed.

Nick was delighted to hear I wanted to remain in L.A. and told me of a similar live-in job he had heard of through his boss, though as a nanny instead of a chauffeur. The position was in Beverly Hills and the interview was that night.

Despite the humor in going from commando to nanny, I leapt at the opportunity. Driving someone's kids to school and vacuuming the living room carpet wasn't fame and fortune, and it certainly wasn't extreme success, but it was a place to live, a car to drive, food in my stomach, and a few dollars to get by on. But more than all that, it was a start. I've since noticed that people striving for extreme success don't consider any task beneath them; they just do whatever it takes.

I went into the interview determined to get that job. My mind wrapped around the task, creating the persona of a successful nanny. Though never having been a nanny or even a baby-sitter, I envisioned the sorts of things a nanny was required to do. When the time came for the interview, the wealthy couple interviewed me together at their enormous Beverly Hills residence. I was very nervous, but need creates performance, and I rose to the task brilliantly. I had an answer for every question. When they admitted that a male nanny was somewhat unusual and made them uncomfortable, I countered that having a former British Paratrooper in the house was guaranteed security—like hiring a nanny and bodyguard at the same time. When they asked if I knew how to iron a proper crease into a dress shirt, I replied that I could iron more precisely than any dry cleaner—British Army training, of course. When they asked if I could clean the house, I explained the concept of military white glove inspections. Finally, as to the subject of references, I sealed the deal by giving them my Army discharge papers showing Exemplary Service, and my parents' phone number to check my upbringing. The next day they called and gave me the job. Talk about your strategy changes—from Central America military adviser to Beverly Hills baby-sitter in a single day. My short-term goals had been a place to sleep and a job. In less than a day, I had a place to sleep, a job, a car, and even a credit card (a gas card for the family's car—again, it was new to me).

Let the record show that the first job I ever performed in America was unloading a dishwasher. It was the first such contraption I'd ever seen.

Perception Means More than Reality

In retrospect, starting as a nanny was the best thing that ever happened to me. I worked for that first household watching over three-year-old Jeffrey for a year, then came time for a change and I went to work for Burt's family as a nanny in Malibu. In Burt I met a savvy businessman willing to mentor his 23-year-old babysitter about how to achieve success. It was Burt, a year or so later, who arranged for me to get my first "proper" job in America. From being a nanny I went to working in Burt's insurance office. The work was steady and challenging, but I realized it would never make me rich.

My first day at work I was asked to place a call to Kentucky, in the 512 area code. After ten tries, I hadn't been able to get through. I asked a co-worker for help. She looked at me like I was a moron after she got through on the first try. As I watched her dial, I realized why: She was dialing a "1" before "512." Needless to say, I'd never made an interstate call before.

I was in awe of Burt, and curious about how he'd come so far in life. So one day I returned to his house and asked him very frankly, "How can I have what you have?"

Burt started by telling me I was lucky to be an immigrant. I was starting at the bottom. I had no place to go but up. Second, not having a safety net like parents or family would give me a better chance to be wealthy because I would never be expecting someone to bail me out. Third, being new to the country gave me a powerful naiveté that freed me from limited thinking and opened my mind to unconventional ways of doing business. "But to really get anywhere," Burt told me in all seriousness, "you've got to work for yourself, start small, and build."

I don't think he thought I'd take that to heart in the manner that I did. Two years later, Kymberly, my girlfriend at the time, and I decided to rent a fence—not the whole fence, actually, just a ten-foot section—at Venice Beach in order to sell T-shirts on the weekends (while working my insurance job during the week). Our goal was to buy T-shirts with minor imperfections from a clothing factory for $2 per shirt, then sell them to the beach crowd for $18. Our display rack was the fence. The guy I rented it from was a brash, direct New Yorker named Howard Gabe. I was nervous that the whopping $1,500 a month I was paying him was too much. I didn't have much money, and blowing it on a fence not only seemed risky, it seemed rather dumb. What had inspired me to rent a fence and sell T-shirts in the first place had been a morning when I walked Venice with Kymberly. I was amazed at the volume of sales by open-air vendors. It was almost manic, the way money changed hands. In that flurry of green, I decided to become an entrepreneur.

But when it came to fork out the cash to rent the fence, I felt foolish. I'd scrimped and saved, watching my money carefully. Giving it away to rent a fence made me feel like I was being taken. I'd already experienced the danger of being gullible in America a year earlier when I gave a man in downtown Los Angeles $50 for a box containing a $500 TV. When I unpacked the box, it was full of telephone books.

I told Howard that I thought he was ripping me off. "Let me see your product," he demanded.

I showed him a few shirts. He appraised them, rubbing the fabric between thumb and forefinger, studying the silk screen designs. "This is good stuff," he said curtly. "Good stuff always sells. How much you charging?"

"Eighteen dollars."

"What're you buying it for?"

"Two dollars."

"You're making sixteen dollars a shirt. You'll do fine. Believe me, you'll be glad you rented this fence."

I was reassured, but only a little. I had heard about New Yorkers. I still saw myself as the immigrant boy trying to make good. That self-perception was limiting me, blinding me to other talents I might possess. Salesmanship, for instance. Subconsciously, I must have known I would make a good salesman or I would never have shelled out the initial month's payment on the fence. But I'd never worked as a salesman, never attended any kind of sales seminar, never read a book on sales techniques. My whole sales technique for those T-shirts was to stand back and hope passers-by liked what they saw. Not much of a technique, really. Why wasn't I taking a more aggressive approach? Because I was scared of rejection and didn't perceive myself as a salesman. It's hard to believe now, because selling is the linchpin holding my business together, but back then I had absolutely no clue I could sell at all.

When the first Saturday of our fence lease came, I went to the beach early with Kymberly and set up a display, hanging shirts on the fence. Venice is a trendy, seedy, funky corner of the universe where street people and movie stars rub shoulders. Inline skaters weave through the crowd, risking life and limb. Music from street performers and boom boxes punctuates the carnival-like atmosphere. On a warm Saturday morning, when Los Angeles heads to the beach, Venice is where they go.

So I knew I wouldn't lack for traffic. Still, my financial investment and perceived lack of salesmanship skills made me nervous. I stood against the fence with Kymberly as the first wave of Saturday morning beach-goers wandered past. My T-shirts told the world I was a salesman, but I stood there with my mouth shut, speaking only when spoken to and nodding politely at all who looked my way.

Kymberly, on the other hand, was California-born and -bred, from a well-to-do business family. She had all the flair and confidence in the world. It was still early, and mostly only joggers and roller skaters were out. After a while, realizing that the shopping crowd came later, she walked off to get coffee for both of us.

As fate would have it, almost as soon as Kymberly left, a young woman roller-skated over to look at the display. I wished Kym were there to deal with her, but standing alone, I mustered up my courage and said hello. She returned the greeting and stared with interest at one of the shirts. "How much?" she asked.

"Uh . . . er . . ." I was embarrassed to tell her the price, fearing she would laugh in my face. "Eighteen dollars."

"Okay," she said quickly, pulling a $20 bill from her

purse. I gave her the shirt and her change in a state of shock. As she skated away, another person came over. Same thing. Kym returned with coffee, shocked to see me holding $36. I was overjoyed, and she laughed at my exuberance. She had always known it would work out.

Without my even knowing it, I became a salesman over the course of the next month, as we sold shirt after shirt. My fears vanquished by success, I learned to chat with everyone who passed by, calling out for people to step over and take a look at the shirts. When people asked the price, I no longer worried it would be too steep. As I relaxed over the next few months and discovered my natural talent for salesmanship, I discovered that even the best salesmen need to use strategies with their clients in order to increase the chances of success. Dealing with people at the street level was the best sales course I could have ever taken. I learned the art of selling on Venice Beach. The same strategies that applied to selling T-shirts apply to selling TV shows. I still use them today.

The first strategy I learned was how to turn a no into a yes. No never means no. It needs to be looked at as merely an objection to overcome. Next I learned the importance of reading people. Customers buy from people they're most comfortable with, people they consider to be their friends. I found that by adjusting my personality to mirror theirs, I could win their confidence and broker a sale. Different personalities respond to different sales techniques, and I broke them into four groups: analytical, emotional, passive, and motivated. Analytical people are engineers, doctors, rocket scientists. These individuals are able to be convinced, and sold, by facts—not hyperbole. When selling something to an analytical person, I provide rational, practical, research-laden reasons for them to buy a product. My delivery is no-nonsense, to the point, and devoid of emotion.

Emotional people, on the other hand, respond to a delivery that drives to the very core of their being. They want feeling. They want passion. Facts make their eyes glaze over. When selling to an emotional person, I would play to that part of the ego driving his or her personality. I might tell a woman how a T-shirt flattered her figure. Or I might tell a man how all the coolest people were wearing this style. In theater, this would be called playing to the audience. In sales, it's giving the customers emotionally what they want. It's just common sense.

The passive customer likes to be dominated, though he would never admit as much. Passive people want to be taken by the hand and told how to behave, told what they like and dislike. They don't like to be bullied, because that preys on the side of their personality that already imagines them a victim. But they do like to be led. Typically, if you lead them to water and remind them they're thirsty, they'll drink. But if you over-aggressively force them to buy they will rebel against you. Passive customers have to be dealt with in a sensitive manner.

The motivated-aggressive customer, on the other

hand, is a leader. He or she wants the salesman to be passive. With that sort of situation I put my ego in my pocket and let the customer be the boss. Did it feel insulting to have someone treat me like their servant? Yes, but I was looking to make a sale, not find intellectual validation. If the motivated-aggressive customer wanted to think he had all the answers, then that was fine with me. These customers want to prove they are right. They're especially easy to sell when they're with a group because they want to show how very smart they are, and what a great financial deal they're getting—even when they can't afford the product. When it comes to making a sale, perception means more than reality.

I made so much money selling T-shirts that I wanted to quit my insurance job. I was making more in a weekend on Venice Beach than in a month at the office. Since Burt had gotten me the insurance job, I owed him the courtesy of asking his permission to leave. However, I was sheepish.

"I hope I haven't let you down by wanting to leave," I told him.

Far from it. Burt was ecstatic. I was making money selling shirts and I was my own boss. "I'm very happy for you. You're on the right track, Mark," Burt told me. "Let me know if I can help you in any way. Let's brainstorm some retail ideas." This reaction reminded me that Burt's way of being positive and seriously happy for the success of others was how I wanted to be. He's been my mentor ever since.

He was right about me being on the right track. I leveraged the money from T-shirt sales into a real estate deal where I made $75,000 in 30 days, then used that money to start my own credit card marketing business. I had become successful. My gut, however, told me there was something missing in my life, though I couldn't quite put my finger on it. I had a home, a nice car, a huge office, and a sizeable bank account. I'd been able to fly home to the East End of London to visit often, the very picture of success. I tried to ignore my nagging inner voice about something missing from the picture, but it wouldn't go away. What, then, was missing?

After attending a dinner party one night I got my answer. I noticed that when I told people I was in the credit card marketing business, they got a bored look in their eyes. This was discouraging, but I felt content in the knowledge that I made plenty of money.

Meanwhile, I overheard a man answering the same question. His job, he told people casually, was movie producer. He had an office over at Columbia Pictures. Now, it's important to note that this guy was no one famous or especially powerful. He hadn't ever produced a movie, and I doubt he had much money to his name. In fact, he got the office and a small stipend for "developing ideas."

But the people at that party couldn't get enough of him and his wonderful job. Men, women, they fell all over this guy. I was unbelievably jealous. The perception that his job was better than mine—despite the reality that I actually produced results and certainly made more money—gave him greater status. I imagined it gave him a greater sense of self-worth, too.

What was it that caused this? It was Hollywood—exciting, glamorous, and the most creative place on earth.

And that's what I was missing: creativity. On the surface, I was jealous of that producer because he was getting more attention. But really, that envy was me thinking I should be doing something in entertainment. He may not actually have been producing, but day in and day out that producer was trying to be creative. He was having an adventure.

Sir Edmund Hillary, the first man to climb Everest, once wrote of a similar epiphany after seeing two men who'd just returned from summiting Mount Cook in New Zealand: "I retreated to a corner of the lounge filled with a sense of the futility of the dull, mundane nature of my existence. Those chaps, now, were really getting a bit of excitement out of life. I decided then and there to take up mountaineering. Tomorrow I'd climb something!"

Or, as Antoine de Saint-Exupéry exhorted others to heed the call of adventure before it was too late: "Now the clay of which you were shaped has dried and hardened, and naught in you will ever awaken the sleeping musician, the poet, the astronomer that possibly inhabited you in the beginning."

The clay of my being had not hardened. Somewhere deep inside me still beat the heart of an adventurer and

I needed to bring it forth before it was too late. Shortly after the dinner party that changed my life, I began looking for ways to leave the credit card business for something a little more stimulating.

Know the Results of Each Day Before It Begins

The screen saver on my laptop reads "Know What Today's Results Will Be." I believe a person can predict results through behavior and should plan their days accordingly. Before going on vacation, for instance, all of our goals are to have a good time. So naturally, we all plan every day of a vacation around doing fun things. At the end of a day we can collapse into bed fulfilled by all the great activities we've done.

So my thought is, why should business be any different? At the start of every day I ask myself what I plan to accomplish before the day is done. Sometimes I write it down, sometimes I keep it in my head. If my goal for a certain day is to create an idea or make a new deal, I gear my behavior and thought process to those outcomes. All my focus, energy, and passion from the time I start working until I shut the lights out and go home is funneled toward that end. I am consumed with accomplishing my daily goal. Nothing is left to chance.

In fact, taking it a step further, I believe you need to act successful to be successful. A controlled confidence both inspires others to follow you and gives a feeling of invincibility that is often needed when things get very tough. One way I get myself to remain confident is by believing that my outcome will always be favorable. I consider my daily goals to already be accomplished, even as I set them. The outcome, then, is known. I just fill in the blanks as it unfolds.

Lots of people have trouble with this approach. They cannot allow themselves this "over-confidence" because they believe they'll jinx themselves and their goals will never come true. I totally disagree. By knowing the outcome of my day I work more efficiently, think more sharply and intuitively. And most of all, I follow through tenaciously until the plan becomes reality. Success is about results, not intentions.

In 1991 I was in Oman, a tiny nation at the southern tip of the Saudi Arabian peninsula, competing in an expedition race with four other teammates. The purpose was to race nonstop across the mountains and deserts for almost 400 miles, staying together as a team at all times. Teams from all over the world were in Oman competing against us, and the starting area, with each team on Arabian horses in a rocky, dry riverbed, had been bedlam. But once we left the horses behind and entered the wilderness on foot the various squads had spread out, until we could no longer see one another. The sensation that my teammates and I were alone in the wilderness was overwhelming. We passed the next several days hearing only the sounds of our footsteps, labored breathing, and assurances to each other that if we kept moving forward—always forward—we would eventually emerge from the wilderness and reach the Arabian Sea where our kayaks were waiting for the next leg of the race.

Oman is a nation basically untouched by modern technology or infrastructure, and as we traveled farther and farther into the Al-Akhbar Mountains, my teammates and I were overcome with the palpable sensation that we had stepped back in time. The terrain was barren, austere, jagged. Our mindset became primitive as the race took us farther and farther from civilization. Our needs were dire and simple: drinking water, food, a soft corner of ground on which to sleep. Amenities like television, fast food, and air-conditioning, which we took for granted back home in Los Angeles, seemed exotic contrivances.

However, one aspect of civilization defined our journey: gear. From our boots to our climbing ropes to our packets of freeze-dried food, my teammates and I were walking, climbing advertisements for the latest in outdoor gear technology. The saying that mankind's ability to reason is what separates us from other species could easily be modified to suit our mindset as we trekked through the daily heat and nightly icebox of Oman. Without our gear, we were one just one step removed from lapsing into the feral mindset of the Bedouins who had patrolled those mountains centuries before.

One day we came to the edge of a cliff. Looking down

from above, I could see the ground 100 meters below. The race organizers had affixed five ropes to the top of the cliff, one for each teammate. We would descend by rappelling. That is, clipping ourselves to the rope, stepping backward off the edge, and carefully lowering ourselves down the face. It is a thrilling task once one gets the hang of it, but the potential for error is always great. Modern technology—gear!—is what makes rappelling possible.

I set my pack on the ground and pulled out the proper equipment for a rappel. On my right hand I slipped a $40 calfskin rappelling glove. On top of my head I set a special helmet that I'd purchased for $100 at a gear store back home. Then I cinched the web climbing harness about my waist and thighs. A special titanium device known as a carabiner was next, clipped through the front of the harness and screwed securely shut so it wouldn't open during the descent. Then a second carabiner as a precautionary measure in case the first one failed. Next, another wonder of modern metallurgy known as a "figure-eight," through which the rope dangling over the edge of the cliff would be threaded to slow my descent.

I clipped the rope, the carabiners, and figure-eight together in the proper configuration, and turned around to gingerly take the first step backward off the edge.

Then, out of nowhere, a little old man appeared. He was a local and couldn't have been a day under 70, and he wore the sheerest of fabrics over his tanned, leathery body and no shoes on his feet. At first I thought he was crazy, because his smile was so broad as he walked briskly to the edge of the cliff. Clearly, he was about to commit suicide.

But then, keeping that same silly grin plastered to his face, that old man grabbed one of the secured ropes and leapt over the edge!! He bounded down that face in seconds. Not walking carefully backward, with the best in modern climbing equipment, as we were about to do, afraid to death of making a fatal mistake—but bounding in massive, joyous leaps. No technology. No gear. Just one barefoot, half-naked old man who had lived alongside the cliff his entire lifetime. I was blown away.

That just goes to show you that results are what's important in life. Not appearance. Not intention. Results. With all the modern technology my teammates and I possessed, none got down that cliff as cleanly as that little old man.

And isn't success the same? Success is about results, not intentions. It's about action, not inertia. It's about wanting something so badly you refuse to quit, no matter what. For instance, people tell me all the time how well they'd do on *Survivor*—but few of them ever fill out an application or send an audition tape. Yes, they dream of winning *Survivor*. But between that dream and successfully cashing the million-dollar check comes hard work, initiative strategy, tenacity, and all the other intangibles defining an individual who does what it takes to succeed. I'm not going to sugarcoat it: Achieving success is not easy. But I will guarantee you that the day you step outside your comfort zone by making success your goal is the day you discover that adversity, risk, and daring will make life sweeter than you ever imagined.

The temptation when the path to success gets too bumpy is to leap back into the comfort zone. Don't. Keep pushing forward, always forward. The comfort zone is the land of dreams and wishes. Success is the land of results, where all those dreams come true.

America is a land made for the disadvantaged because here results count the most. Back in Europe, oftentimes family influence, the right schooling, or connections are a prerequisite to even getting the opportunity to try. But Americans will give everyone a chance to try. I always remember that as long as I'm willing to try, I'll still have a chance to deliver results. The results of the ensuing effort are all that matter.

Have the Courage to Fail (If You're Not Failing, You're Not Taking Enough Risks)

VERY OFTEN I'M ASKED what motivates me to keep asking more of myself in my business and personal life. My answer is always honest, outlining rogue visions of how I want to continue reinventing television, goals I've yet to accomplish, and adventures still over the horizon. But really, those are just symptoms of my hunger for a higher level of personal fulfillment through success. What gets me up in the morning (and keeps me up late nights) is a symbiotic pair of catalysts.

The first catalyst is the euphoria of success. The intensely fulfilling sensation of success blankets doubt and quiets naysayers. Hours of hard work and sacrifice are recounted with revel and idealized for the virtues they are. Life feels sublime. A glow emanates from your being.

Is it any wonder success is so addictive?

The second catalyst, however, is far less romantic. It's

my deep, deep fear of failure. My approach to life means I take risks and think outside the box every single day. By their very nature, those activities constitute a flirtation with failure. That two-syllable reminder of negative consequences is the most reviled word in the lexicon of success, but as unavoidable for risk-takers as death and taxes. I am afraid of failure and all it implies, but I have made it a catalyst for success by spinning this fear 180 degrees, into a positive learning tool. When I do fail, I rehash the events leading up to it. Like a football coach studying film of a losing game, I examine which strategies worked and which didn't. I question my attitudes, comments, and commitment. I pinpoint the precise cause of that failure and vow never to let it happen again. The second (or third or fourth) time around, success invariably results. In a very weird way, failure is my friend—and should be yours, too.

I'll even admit to taunting failure on occasion. A case in point is my habit of verbalizing goals. Some people believe you should never discuss something you plan to do. They think that talking out loud about an idea or dream will make others jealous, cause unnecessary negative feelings, make it not come true, rob the goal of its energy.

I believe the opposite. If I have a new idea, I talk about it all the time. I chat with people about the idea, much the same way I pitched *Survivor* at dinner parties. My friends and business associates inevitably have an opinion on what I'm thinking of doing. Through their feedback I puzzle over the idea, sharpen it. The goal gathers energy. Over the centuries, humans have created great technologies through such a sharing of ideas. I like to think I'm carrying on a long tradition of discourse.

Obviously, the drawback to such verbalizing is public ridicule if I fail. That's why I think many people are reluctant to talk about their hopes and dreams and ideas. Not because saying it aloud will jinx it, but because they're afraid people will laugh at them if they fail. Well, you know what? There will always be people standing on the sideline, hoping you fail because they're afraid to take risks of their own. The Australians call this the "Tall Poppy" syndrome—all the poppies are jealous of the one that grows tallest and strive to cut it back down to size.

Know this: If you do fail, they'll be the first to spread the word. It's been my experience, however, that in America the number of people cheering you on when you finally succeed greatly outnumbers that small crowd mocking you when you don't.

Dare to be a tall poppy. Chase your dreams. Shout them to the world if you feel brave enough. And when you get discouraged, remember that only in wartime is failure fatal.

Take Risks and Dream Big

One of the greatest freedoms of living in America is being able ask the question: "If I could do anything I wanted with my life—money being no object—what would I do?" In many parts of the world, people don't have the luxury of asking that question. They are societally bound to an occupation their entire life, with no hope of the education, transportation, or the financial wherewithal necessary to break out. Think of all the untapped potential going to waste. How many would-be Einsteins, Picassos, and Mozarts are laboring in rice paddies or in sweatshops, their gifts and internal fire withering day by day until they finally vanish?

That's sad. But really, what's even more sad are men and women who have the opportunity to do anything—anything!—with their life, but are so afraid of failure and ridicule they never venture beyond their comfort zone. I'm reminded of the Oscar Wilde maxim that "a man is never old until regrets take the place of dreams." Really, that should never happen. Regrets are a fact of life, but dreams burn brightly as long as we're willing to take the hard risks needed to make them come true. I know this from experience.

By 1991 I'd finally achieved a level of success in America. Less than a decade after arriving, I had a home, a nice car, and a burgeoning banking business. I no longer woke up dreading that I was on the verge of ruin. So it was that I lay in bed the morning of February 21, lingering over the *Los Angeles Times*. A color photo caught my eye, that of a canoe paddling through a dank jungle canal. The water was opaque, and it didn't take much imagination to realize that wasn't the type of place one went for a swim.

Always attracted to adventure and wild places, I focused on the article. In vivid prose, the writer detailed a French adventure competition known as the Raid Gauloises. The Raid was held in a different exotic country every year, and that particular year the location was Costa Rica. The goal was for five-person teams, each having at least one woman, to race nonstop over mountains, down rivers, and through jungles so snake-infested that teams carried their own supply of antivenin. Their modes of transportation for this stage race were trekking, horseback, rafting, kayaking, whitewater rafting, and even parachuting. At one spot during the Costa Rica race, teams hiked 20 miles through a crocodile refuge.

The races lasted up to two weeks and covered several hundred miles. Teams carried all their own food, water, and gear. They slept just an hour per night. It reminded me so much of my parachute regiment days, just without the weapons; it seemed the perfect competition to indulge the side of me that enjoys hardship. I once read a quotation from an Eskimo named Igjugardik: "All the true wisdom is to be found far from the dwellings of man, in the great solitudes, and can only be attained through suffering. Suffering and privation are the only things that can open the mind of man to that which is hidden from his fellows."

I have come to totally believe in this.

The "expedition racing" concept wasn't new to me. The people of New Zealand are famous for their love of outdoor adventure, and I had read articles about similar races being held through the glaciers and fiords of New Zealand's Southern Alps. The French race was sprung from that concept. But reading the *Times* that morning, I suddenly became consumed with an idea: I should launch an expedition-length race of my own in the United States. I'd seen research showing that the three dominant themes of the 90s would be the environment, extreme sports, and self-actualization through challenge. No other format combined all three like expedition racing.

My race would be called the Eco-Challenge, I decided. Interestingly, the gestation period from idea to actuality would be four years, the same amount of time it would someday take to bring *Survivor* to life.

My first step toward making Eco-Challenge happen came when I contacted Gerard Fusil, the Frenchman coordinating the Raid Gauloises, and signed him as a consultant in spring of 1991. He would be my insurance policy. In my mind's eye, the outcome of this endeavor was clear: a safe, rigorous Eco-Challenge expedition race, with a stunning television production beamed into homes shortly thereafter. Competitors would praise Eco for its organization and physical challenge. The broad impact of television would soon have every man, woman, and child in America thinking the words *adventure* and *Eco-Challenge* synonymously. The first Eco would lead to a second and a third and a fourth, as well as merchandising, a travel company, and international franchising of the event.

That business goal became the driving force in my life. I had come to a point in my life, however, where I needed to define myself by more than just business relationships and accomplishments. I craved action and adventure, two constants in my life when I was a paratrooper. I wanted to experience once again that place Charles Lindbergh described as "beyond the descriptive words of men . . . where man is more than man, and existence both supreme and valueless at the same instant."

Too often in society linear, black-and-white thinking dictates that certain arenas are oxymoronic. So it was with adventure and business. My goal was to prove that thinking absurd. Not only did I think the two blended together perfectly, their pairing also had a pure, organic quality—the primal and modern sides of my personality merging to show me my potential.

As part of my strategy for launching Eco-Challenge I took an unusual step. I would race in the Raid Gauloises. This would show me how my future customers actually felt while racing, and help me become a better race producer. With the 1992 Raid scheduled to be held in the fall in the Arab country of Oman, I had roughly seven months to find a team, acquire the financial sponsorship necessary to pay the entry fee and cover travel costs, and transform my body back into the hardened steel of a British Paratrooper's. It would be a total body makeover entailing weight training, dietary adjustments, running, kayaking, and rock climbing. I would become better, smarter, faster. I tried to persuade myself my credit card marketing business would be an ongoing concern, but my gut told me that it would go by the wayside. At that time, during the savings and loan crisis, I had decided to try to buy a savings and loan and issue secured credit cards to Spanish-speaking citizens who otherwise lacked the documentation to gain a traditional credit card. The research was going extremely well, and it seemed like it could be a big moneymaker, but my inner voice told me I didn't have the mental or emotional energy to be a banker and an adventurer at the same time.

If you want to know what it feels like to have dreams ridiculed, you should have been in my shoes back then. People thought I was crazy. They told me so. There I was, finally on the brink of financial security after a decade of struggle, about to realize even bigger life success, giving it up to chase a life of adventure. Friends were very kind when I explained about expedition racing and Eco-Challenge and my grand plan to make Eco an international brand name. They listened to my grand schemes and nodded their heads politely and remarked how they wished they had the courage to attempt something so bold. Many, however, also made it plain that at 32 years old I was having an early midlife crisis. Or that I was sabotaging my chances at success. I heard my name associated with the Peter Pan syndrome more than once.

But really, what's so wrong with Peter Pan? Peter Pan flies. He is a metaphor for dreams and faith. Some would disparage Peter Pan for his youthful exuberance, but I would need his qualities in epic proportions to finish the Raid Gauloises, then make my Eco-Challenge soar.

My naiveté shone like a beacon as I prepared to race the Raid. On the negative side, that dynamic led me to choose my teammates poorly—among them a stockbroker, an actor, and a personal trainer. They were good people and gym fit, but lacked outdoor adventure skills. I realized that when I selected them, but thought it could be overcome if I shared my British Army training with them. In actuality, I should have realized that I needed teammates with greater outdoor skills than I, not lesser.

I lined up a lucrative series of corporate sponsors to back my team and jumpstart my Eco-Challenge corporation. I promised them media attention as return on their investment. To fulfill that obligation I cold-called media outlets, pitching the story of my plucky team. Now I know better. But back then I thought that's how it was done. Incredibly, it worked. *Runner's World* magazine agreed to do a feature story based solely on my exuberant pitch to their editor. The writer contracted to write the piece told me he'd never heard of such a thing happening before.

On a more career-oriented note, a Los Angeles television station agreed to send a camera crew to Oman to film a one-hour special on our race. I brashly stipulated that I wanted to share in their sponsorship revenue for

the special. The station agreed. I still can't believe it. I—
a total television novice—would be getting sponsorship
dollars for a special being aired in the most influential
media market in the world. And all I had to do was ask.

In that unlikely manner, I made my entrance into the
television and sponsorship industries.

In November, my teammates and I (our name was
Team American Pride) flew to the medieval land of
Oman. The tiny nation on the Arabian Sea featured
daunting desert and mountain topography, blistering
days and frigid nights, dead-end canyons, and riverbeds
prone to flash flooding. It seemed an ideal location for
a wilderness competition. Outside the capital city of
Muscat, there was little in the way of modern amenities
or population. Indeed, I sensed the country had
changed little since Biblical times.

My teammates and I were awed by Oman, and by the
wiry physiques of our fellow competitors. I was nervous
and more than a little intimidated. The pressures of being a first-time competitor, first-time subject of a television show, and the first-time responsibility of satisfying
sponsors weighed heavily on me in the days leading up
to the race. I endured the anxious thoughts of the un-
proven: Am I good enough? Am I deluding myself by
thinking I can pull this off? Am I in over my head? I
fought them by remembering all the hours of preparation leading up to the race. Another morale boost came
at the pre-race briefing, where race coordinator Gerard
Fusil introduced each team individually. He reminded

the international assemblage that American Pride was the first U.S. team to compete in the Raid Gauloises, which led to a raucous cheer and prolonged applause. My spirits soared.

Personal validation and the acceptance of peers are vital to all endeavors, which is why Fusil's simple announcement was so powerful. The cheering and applause warmed me, motivated me, relaxed me. I'd been welcomed back into the elite circle of men and women who call themselves adventurers. My doubts were behind me. I was filled with optimism about the race. Team American Pride would be the surprise of the field. I was sure of it.

And we were. But not the sort of surprise I'd envisioned.

We rose at 3:30 race morning to prepare for the predawn start. The Raid would begin with 20 miles of horseback riding, then we would dismount and trek 50 miles through the Jebel Akdar mountain range. After that would come kayaking on the Arabian Sea, another mountain trekking section, then a 60-mile camel ride.

"It was pitch-black at the starting line," I wrote in my journal that first morning. Fusil had directed each team to approach the corral and select their mounts, though finding it in the darkness was an event unto itself. "And we were all stumbling over a very rocky, dry riverbed toward the sound of whinnying horses."

In what would be the first of many mistakes, we selected our horses poorly. When the gun sounded, sending 51 teams pell-mell up the riverbed, we fell behind immediately. Our horses were lame and stubborn. One nag refused to let us ride her; we had to drag her the entire 36 kilometers. While the fastest teams took just three and a half hours to reach the waterfalls of Snake Canyon, end of the horseback section, Team American Pride took over twelve.

We immediately leapt from the horses and began the difficult roped ascent up through the waterfalls of Snake Canyon. Frigid water beat on our heads, drenched us, brought forth the early stages of hypothermia. At the top we encountered more water as we navigated the narrow canyon, alternately running the rocky trails and swimming icy pools in the dark. The adventure was truly hardcore, and we made it more difficult because we had packed too much. Each of us carried a 70-pound pack, whereas the more expert teams carried a mere 20 pounds. The French literally sneered at our loads.

When we finally got some momentum, however, another setback: One of my teammates refused to continue racing until we built a fire and dried our clothes. With time of the essence, I thought his request absurd. We argued. The night was cold and the sky filled with stars. Under normal circumstances the beauty would have been dazzling. But I was frozen, wet, tired, hungry, and bristling with rage; the beauty was lost on me.

I lost the argument. We built a fire and waited until morning before continuing. Team American Pride had ceased to be a competitive squad. We were now in Oman just to tour the course.

Our entire race became a downward spiral from hope and optimism to miserable failure. Inexperience and mismatched personalities, combined with raw weather and my own poor navigation, forced my team to fracture when things got tough. One time we were so low on water we had to take turns drinking the last sip from our canteen, swirling it around our mouths, then spitting it back into the canteen and passing it to the next teammate.

The defining moment of the ordeal occurred during the kayaking leg. We were paddling parallel to the coast, a mile off shore, when a storm struck. The skies grew black, the ocean surface became a nauseating undulation of six-foot swells, and the wind blew so hard that salt spray stung like shards of glass as it was shoved against our exposed faces. Navigation was nearly impossible. The air filled with rescue helicopters (though teams faced disqualification by being rescued). Sharks circled. "The storm was huge," I wrote later in my journal. "To be honest, I think the only reason we got through it was because we were all so scared."

Not all of us got through it, though. When the storm was at its worst, the same teammate who'd insisted on building the fire a few nights before panicked. He abruptly announced that he wanted to quit, or at least rest on shore until the storm passed. The team told him he was crazy. As Southern Californians, our strong suit was ocean kayaking, and we had the ideal opportunity to make up distance between us and other teams. Furthermore, the beach was being pounded by huge breakers. He could die if he tried to paddle through them. For his safety and the team's, I forbade him to go ashore.

In an act of mutiny, my teammate paddled hard toward the shore. Since Raid rules dictate that all five members must travel and finish together or be disqualified, he was effectively negating our months of training and hard work. The rest of us paddled on without him.

One of the rescue helicopters found my teammate washed up on the beach, asleep and dazed. When asked if he knew our whereabouts, he shrugged and answered he had no idea. It was assumed we were lost at sea. When this news was radioed back to Fusil on the shore at Wadi Shab, one of the largest manhunts in Raid history began. No one had ever died during a Raid, and it seemed a cruel act of fate for the first-time American team to be the first. Out of desperation, Fusil set aloft in a search and rescue helicopter to look for us.

He never found us. Instead, we paddled through the afternoon. Unbeknownst to us, we were the only team still out on the ocean. We spent the night with locals in a small fishing village. As we beached our kayaks, about 100 children helped us pull the heavy kayaks the 100 meters to get above the high tide line that would come later that evening. The local fishermen then ran their hands along our sleek craft, examining every aspect of their design. It turned out they had never seen fiberglass boats.

An impromptu feast followed, as they shared their food with us and we spent a wonderful cultural Arabic evening. We slept briefly, then put to sea at dawn and paddled on through the early morning light, not knowing that Raid organizers had canceled the kayaking section due to weather. When we arrived at Wadi Shab at noon, Fusil was so relieved he celebrated. "The Americans have arrived. The Americans have arrived!" he cried joyfully.

There was no celebrating, however, when we confronted our renegade teammate. Now clean and shaved, he came out to greet us as our boats kissed the shore. Because of the storm's ferocity, and more importantly, because he wanted the publicity associated with an American team finishing the race, Fusil had decided to bend the rules and let him rejoin us so that our team could continue officially. The four of us remembered his selfishness and mutiny all too well. Looking our former teammate in the eye, we told him one by one that we wouldn't take him back. Then we shouldered our packs and continued the race, unofficially as an incomplete team of four.

A second team member withdrew due to injury a few days later, but I continued the race with my two remaining teammates and a group of athletes whose teams had also splintered. We were French, Japanese, and American; exhausted, smelly, hungry, driven by the desire to finish what we started.

After 10 days, 1 hour, and 15 minutes, we arrived at Checkpoint 22, which, due to the cancellation of the final camel leg (on account of uncontrollable camels) had become the official finish line. With me were Susan and Norman, my surviving American Pride teammates. We all cried, then we celebrated with cold French champagne, hot showers, and a good night's sleep. Even as the sublime sensation of accomplishment washed over us, however, I began a mental study of what I had done wrong. First, I'd chosen my team poorly. I needed professional adventurers. Second, I'd been a poor manager. I have a talent for outdoor adventure, but my strengths are coordination, macro-management, and deal-making. There's no way I should have been the navigator, micro-managing every last moment of the race. On an ideal team, I would bring an experienced team together, then cede control during the race to an individual with better tactical and navigational skills.

The failure nagged at me. What would I tell the sponsors? How would this affect Eco-Challenge? Before my plane home was halfway over the Atlantic, I had my answers. I would learn from my failure to keep my epic dream alive. I think that's the day I realized that Eco-Challenge and the world of adventure was how I was destined to spend my life. No longer was I just an immigrant trying to scrap his way to the top. No. I had a niche. I had a dream. I had learned a hard, invaluable lesson. I would not let my dream die. It was imperative that I finished the Raid as a means of establishing credibility. (Years later, when my staff began calling me The Method Producer for my need to personally pre-race every Eco-Challenge course to know what competitors would feel, one young producer noted that would be like an actor getting shot before filming a gunshot scene so he could better know the sensation.)

What was I going to do? Go back to the Raid—and win. The 1993 Raid was being held in Madagascar, a barren moonscape where crocodiles filled the rivers and temperatures shattered the thermometer. I had a year to assemble a crack team and increase my fitness to my greatest level ever if I was going to win. Mentally, even though I would be reviewing videotape of Oman in the days and months ahead while preparing the television special, I needed to set aside the disaster and focus on Madagascar.

Not only did I want to win the Raid for my only personal reasons of adventure, I was going back with the intention of producing another television show about my Raid experience. This time, however, I wanted the Madagascar show to air nationally so that potentially everyone in America would have a vicarious taste of expedition racing, and in so doing, it would make it easier to secure a national television deal for Eco-Challenge when the time came. I felt ESPN would be the perfect outlet for Madagascar. The question was how to go about it.

Keep Cool, Even When Things Are Most Dire

Failure can have a domino effect. Unless it is seen as a tool for growth and future success, the emotional toll of failure erodes confidence and optimism. A low-grade panic sets in when it becomes obvious nothing is going right. That panic turns to a fear that every action of every day in every arena will be fraught with imminent screw-ups. It's the Midas touch, only in reverse.

Failure gives you time to gather yourself, take a deep breath, and remind yourself that the past is the past. It's done. Learn and move on. To do that, you've got to keep cool. No matter how bad things get, you must always make calm, level-headed decisions. Giving in to adrenaline and fear will turn a potential success into a failure every time. The long-term stigma of panic under pressure, temper tantrums, moping, whining, and rage-filled outbursts is the perception of weakness—and weakness is one of the two most unappealing traits known (the other is quitting). You may forget how you behaved when the going got tough, but others won't.

In 1993, while training for the Madagascar Raid, my teammate Susan—the lone holdover from the Oman squad—along with myself and my three new teammates, went skydiving over the Southern California desert. I hadn't skydived since my Army days ten years earlier, but it was a Raid discipline and I needed to brush up on my skills. Luckily, my three new teammates were Navy

SEAL commandos I'd recruited specially for the Raid—Bruce Schliemann, Pat Harwood, and the ever-capable Rick was a SEAL skydiving instructor. It was reassuring to know that, in event of an emergency, the three of them would find a way to make things right.

We leapt from the plane at 13,000 feet, then linked arms and fell in formation until we reached 5,000 feet. If you've ever skydived, you know the intense rush of dropping from the sky at 140 miles per hour. The freedom of fight merges with an unsettling terror that something, somehow, will go wrong. I love the romance of leaping from a plane but am too much of a realist to deny that it scares me like few other adventurous undertakings. In the parachute regiment, I had seen parachutes fail to open properly; seen the mess of broken legs and spleens that accompanied even a minor malfunction; heard about the craters made by bodies hitting the ground after two-mile freefalls. It is my fervent desire that this never happens to me.

One by one, we separated from the formation to release our pilot chutes. Pat and Bruce separated first. I reached for my own pilot chute and I assumed Rick had already done the same, making me the last one still freefalling. I placed my hand on my right hip and pulled the rubber ball that would release my pilot chute, which would then release my main chute.

Nothing happened. The pilot chute, that small drogue that precedes the main chute to insure an orderly opening, was stuck. Even as the ground raced toward me, I reached again and tried to tug the pilot chute free. No joy.

Needless to say, that was a pretty desperate situation. Out of the corner of my eye, I noticed Rick still freefalling. When he saw I was in trouble, he delayed pulling his own chute and risked his life to help me. He was using his body as an aerodynamic platform to fly to my assistance. What a guy!

So we're freefalling, unable to speak because of the wind, and communicating through facial expression and sign language. Rick mimed pulling his ripcord, asking me what was wrong. I pointed to the pilot chute. He could see that it was stuck, then he motioned that he would fly closer and pull it for me. That's a dangerous maneuver under any conditions, but even more dangerous so close to the ground. If we were to accidentally smack into each other, one or both of us could have been knocked unconscious, or become entangled as my chute deployed.

I shook my head and motioned for him to back off. Whatever happened, I would do it myself.

I pointed to my reserve chute. I'd been reluctant to pull the reserve for two reasons: First, if the pilot chute finally came loose after the reserve was already open, I'd have two chutes. They would tangle. So close to the ground, that would be fatal.

Second, pulling the reserve is a last-ditch maneuver and should only be done in an emergency. That's when a little voice inside my head calmly reminded me that *this* was an emergency. I needed to pull the reserve and pull it immediately.

I nodded to Rick, who understood. He changed his body attitude so that he tracked away from me. I checked my altometer. I had fallen 10,000 feet and was now at only 3,000 feet. It was now or never—I pulled my reserve. It opened with a hard thud, and blossomed into the most wonderful sight: a lime-green, fully formed chute. What a glorious, welcome sight. I floated safely to the ground, awash in the euphoria of being alive, but also racked by the post-adrenaline-jag questions of "what if?" What if I'd been unable to open the reserve chute? What if Rick and I had become tangled? What if, what if, what if?

As Rick landed close by, I was struck by the realization that, by all rights, I should have been panicked up there. But I had reminded myself over and over to stay calm. Being panicked only adds to the self-perception that things are out of control. If I'd panicked up in the sky nothing fruitful would have come from it, and I'm sure I would have left a hole in the ground.

In a strange way I was thankful for the trial by fire. You never know if you'll be able to remain calm and thinking clear in a quickly approaching death situation. By remaining calm I proved to my new teammates that when push came to shove, I had the right stuff. More important, I knew I could trust myself, as well.

That trust became crucial during the Madagascar race. Late in the race we undertook a 40-hour nonstop walk across a desert known as the Mikea Forest (*forest* being a misnomer, referring ambitiously to a thick swath of thorny scrub). The lead teams were just hours ahead and we were sure the forced march would catapult us to victory. The daytime temperature was a ferocious 135 degrees—so hot that French journalists reported it ten degrees cooler in their dispatches home for fear no one would believe them. The nighttime sections of that trek were cool and beautiful, lit by a full moon. We were exhausted; our pace was slow but steady as we trudged through a sparse forest.

The pygmies surrounded us just past midnight. There were at least 30 of them. The French had told us of a mythic tribe of little people living in the Mikea Forest, but we had assumed it was just local legend, like fairies in regions of the English countryside.

These men, however, were very real, stood just two feet away, and had us completely surrounded. The hard looks on their faces betrayed hostile intent no less effectively than the spears leveled toward the five of us. They said nothing, and wore tunics of the brightest red fabric, which made me think of Central Africa's Masai warriors. The combination of the husky moon, red tunics, spears, pygmies, and my thorough exhaustion made the moment surreal beyond words. I might have thought I was hallucinating if I hadn't heard Rick and Pat discussing ways to defend ourselves. "I'm taking the safety off on my pencil flare," Rick said, speaking of the emergency illumination provided by race organizers.

Per race rules, we had no weapons of any kind. A flare would have to do in a pinch.

"Okay. Me, too," Pat said. "I'll take the ones on the left."

It was second-nature for my SEAL teammates to lapse into a military posture, and I could see clearly that they were trying to make the best of a threatening situation. We were outnumbered six to one in this showdown. But even if Pat and Rick and Bruce managed to take out a handful of men, that left plenty of angry pygmies to finish us off. Clearly, something else was needed.

I looked at the spear of the man standing before me, then slowly—an inch per second—I began extending my right hand toward the tip. The warrior could see what I was doing, but made no attempt to stop me. He just watched. Perhaps he thought I was a fool.

Soon the other pygmies began watching my hand's journey toward the razor-sharp spear. There was no turning back. All eyes were soon on me, even those of my teammates. What in the world, they had to be wondering, was Burnett up to? Was he trying to get himself killed?

I extended my forefinger as if to point. The warrior's muscles clenched and he held the spear tight. Delicately, I pressed my finger against the point as if testing its sharpness—and man, it was sharp.

I had crossed the point of no return. Either my strategy was about to save the day or I was about to look like a total moron, and get a spear through my gut.

I pulled my finger back quickly, howled in great comic pain, then collapsed to the ground as if shot. I rolled around on the ground and continued to scream in pain. I like to think I looked like Steve Martin doing one of his exaggerated comic bits. My rationale was a bit more measured—I figured we seemed as odd to the pygmies as they seemed to us. I hoped to defuse the tension by showing we weren't a threat.

For a moment my howling was the only sound echoing off that dark desert. Then one pygmy laughed, and another, and another. Soon all the pygmies had burst out in uproarious laughter. They'd never seen such a foolish man in all their lives. Spears were lowered, relieved exhales were emitted by my teammates. We ended up explaining with sign language and dirt drawings about a lake we were trying to find. Once they understood they motioned for us to follow and we spent the next three hours traipsing through the Madagascan night with our new friends. They led us directly to the edge of the Mikea Forest that bordered our lake, then with a last smile they disappeared back into the forest, gone forever.

Keeping cool, even when things were dire, is not always the obvious course of action. But I'm living proof it's the best.

Never Quit

Rick, Pat, Susan, Bruce, and I finished ninth in Madagascar. We were the first American team to officially complete the Raid, and our ninth-place finish was very respectable. After our trek across the desert we arrived on the Mozambique Channel, slept two incredibly short hours in the fishing village of Andavadoaka, then kayaked two days nonstop to the finish line. We hallucinated as we paddled, and fell asleep mid-stroke, so great was our fatigue.

I'd set aside my micromanaging ways and given control of the team to Rick Holman. He'd done a fantastic job. And rather than be disappointed we hadn't won the Raid, the first thing I did after a hot shower and very long sleep was to figure out what we did wrong—and how we could do better. The team had performed phenomenally. There was no reason to think the same squad wasn't capable of winning the 1994 Raid, which was scheduled to be held in the jungles of Borneo. At the prize ceremony, Gerard Fusil, the Raid organizer I'd paid to consult on developing the Eco-Challenge, told the assembled competitors that my Team American Pride was "very dangerous, watch out for them next year."

As well as managing to finish ninth and make a little history by becoming the first American team to finish, I had also managed to convince KCAL Channel 9 in Los Angeles to pay to send their on-air sports reporter, Mark Steines, to Madagascar to produce a one-hour special about the exploits of our team. It was my second venture into pulling together a television deal and this one was significantly better than my Oman deal. I had convinced the Raid Gauloises organizers to provide me free copies of all the footage their ten camera crews would shoot at the Madagascar Raid, in return for which I would get the Raid Gauloises publicized on American TV. The other side of this deal was that I convinced KCAL to accept this footage and have Mark Steines edit it, at KCAL's cost, into a one-hour special. The Raid was happy to have gotten an American show and KCAL was happy to end up with a one-hour show that would have cost over a million dollars had they shot it themselves.

But the best part of the entire deal was that KCAL would only get to air this show once, then the show became my property to distribute. I had simultaneously arranged a deal with ESPN to accept the KCAL one-hour show. Essentially, they were acquiring free programming. In return ESPN would provide me with 30 percent of the commercial minutes available during their broadcast. I then sold these commercial minutes to my Team American Pride sponsors. Looking back, it was a pretty audacious scenario, but it worked and the ESPN show got fairly good ratings. I had definitely begun to learn how to be bold and creative in putting together a national television deal. I knew that these newfound skills would serve me well later.

Since this early adventure in Madagascar, Mark Steines has moved on to national prominence as an anchor on *Entertainment Tonight,* and we have become close friends. He often still laughs with disbelief that KCAL, the Raid, and ESPN agreed to my crazy deal.

. . .

I LET MY RACING SUCCESS in Madagascar and my national television deal go to my head and decided to race again in 1994, so I could go for the win. Big mistake. My focus needed to shift. It could no longer be racing the Raid, as it had been the past two years. That chapter of my life should have been done. It was time to turn my energies from six months of training and racing each year, into making my dream of an Eco-Challenge come true. I'd done the research, endured the hardship of actually racing, observed the logistical nightmares of Raid officials as they struggled to keep track of 50 teams spread over hundreds of miles of wilderness. I admired their hard work, but also knew I had to greatly improve on their methods. American racers would expect flawless execution. Also, any TV company that financed me would expect American-quality production. I planned to produce an efficient Eco-Challenge and more than double the number of film crews covering the race. I had a gut awareness that the future of Eco-Challenge depended on television. I intended to produce a dynamic show about racers questing after this Holy Grail. I wanted Eco to be more epic, more dramatic, more bombastic—a David Lean film come to life. I'd learned what I needed to learn by racing. I should have moved on. But I was stupid and decided to take on both racing in Borneo and simultaneously producing the first Eco-Challenge.

I immersed myself in raising money, finding a course location, and convincing teams to come race Eco. I was irked that people kept comparing it with the Hawaiian

Ironman competition, when, in fact, Eco-Challenge
was far tougher. In response, I ran a two-page advertisement in *Triathlete* magazine that said "This Little
Race Eats Ironmen For Breakfast." Such confidence
made me an easy target for those in the endurance racing world. They questioned my ability to make such a
claim, particularly since I hadn't ever competed in
Ironman. My response was always that I'd completed
two Raids, though I knew that wasn't enough pedigree
to quiet the most savage critics. More than ever, I
wanted to win the Raid Gauloises to show I had the
right stuff. Since even Ironman competitors grudgingly
agreed the Raid was the toughest race on earth at the
time, winning would mean never again having my
toughness questioned.

The problem was that I was immersed 24 hours a day,
7 days a week, living, eating, and sleeping my development of Eco-Challenge. But I wasn't training properly
for the Raid. When I arrived in Borneo for my third and
final attempt to win the Raid Gauloises, I was mentally
still home in Southern California preparing for Eco.
Making matters more daunting, the Raid field was the
toughest in history. If Team American Pride was going
to win, it would take a supreme effort.

We flew from Los Angeles to Kuching, a tourist town
on the island's northern coast. As always, I arranged
for sponsors to finance the cost of flying the team and
to provide all the team equipment and food. Just the
fact of raising the sponsorship money, arranging the

logistics, trying to train, and trying to develop Eco-Challenge had me arriving in Kuching mentally and physically exhausted. I needed a vacation, not an endurance race.

From Kuching, it was a 17-hour odyssey to the starting area via turboprop; express boat (a sleek, enclosed passenger boat resembling a DC-10 without wings) that reeked of insecticide; four-wheel-drive jeep; and a ten-mile trek through the rain forest. The Raid contingent of athletes, journalists, and assistance crews marched in a single-file line—over 500 people in all.

The deluge began early in our hike. Water gushed from the heavens as if shot from a fire hose, and every inch of me was soaked. There was so much water in my hiking boots that it was spilling over. The ground was a mud yellow like mustard and slick as ice. Walking uphill meant stooping on all fours and using roots and tree trunks as makeshift ladder rungs. Walking downhill was worse, and I'm sure I spent more of it sliding on my backside than actually trekking. The rain and mud-smeared clothing diminished my resolve even further. I dreaded the upcoming race, scheduled to start the following dawn.

As luck would have it, we arrived at our destination of Ba Kelalan just as the rain stopped. The village was small, just an airstrip, school, and scattered huts. The local children serenaded us as we marched in, their angelic voices and scrubbed faces in sharp contrast to the sodden, weary competitors.

My teammates and I stowed our gear on the hard-wood floor of a schoolroom. It was not luxurious, but a roof over our heads would be welcome when the inevitable midnight monsoon struck. An Australian team shared the space. Between the two squads, the level of nervous energy was stifling.

I needed to get out, be alone, clear my head. I went for a walk, trying all the while to figure out how I'd gotten myself so emotionally detached from the enormous undertaking I was about to embark upon. Even though I'd done the Raid twice, it clearly wasn't going to be any easier the third time around. If anything, given my distraction, it would be much more strenuous. I knew the Raid would mean days and nights of immense suffering. There would be endless confrontations with personal fear as we trekked through claustrophobic jungle choked with leeches, wild pigs, cobras, and man-eating reticulated pythons. I don't know how I fooled myself into thinking I would finish, let alone win, but I did.

But even as I tried to summon passion for my teammates and the race, my mind wandered back to my office, and the thousands of phone calls I needed to make if Eco was to become a reality. I interrupted my walk time and again to tell other teams about this exciting new American event, the Eco-Challenge. It would be held in April, 1995, just six months after the Borneo Raid. The title sponsor was Hi-Tec Sports, the same company sponsoring Team American Pride.

Right up to the moment the gun sounded I was soliciting other teams to come race Eco. I was a lone man on a mission, justifying my actions by seeing the big picture: The Raid was very small in the big scheme of things, but Eco was my stepping-stone to greatness. I can't blame myself for that point of view, but I also can't find fault with my teammates for the animosity they expressed. Clearly, I was in Borneo for Mark Burnett, not Team American Pride.

When we finally got under way, animosity was replaced by optimism. My entire team expected to win. I finally set aside thoughts of Eco. My 40-pound pack felt uncomfortable on my back as we trekked quickly from a small clearing into the jungle. Sunlight went from being an equatorial spotlight to being filtered, and almost blotted out, by the green canopy. My Navy SEAL triad of Rick Holman, Pat Harwood, and Bruce Schliemann were navigating. Then—and I don't know the precise moment it occurred, but I remember thinking it was awfully early in the Raid for such a thing to happen—we were lost. The 1994 Raid Gauloises was ten minutes old. We were supposed to be looking for a trail that would take us up a mountainside. Instead, we were utterly, completely lost, stumbling off-trail through wall after wall of vegetation. The confusion of being lost in the jungle is mind-boggling. There are no landmarks to orient north, south, east, or west. Maps are basically useless. Forward movement means hacking trail with a machete—arm-numbing work that brings exhaustion quickly in hot equatorial climates.

We despaired when darkness fell and we hadn't seen another team in almost 20 hours. We endured the terror of marching all night through primitive jungle, never quite sure whether those pink eyes reflecting from our head lamps were going to attack. In all that time, we didn't hear or see another team. Finally, at noon on the second day of the race, we entered a small village nestled in a clearing. Our joy was beyond words.

Then we looked around. Everything looked so familiar. The houses, the airstrip, the school . . . we were back in Ba Kelalan!!!

We had walked in a circle. The Raid Gauloises was 24 hours ahead of us. Why had I wasted my time coming?

The smart thing to do in that situation would have been to review what I already knew about the Raid—that 24-hour gaps can be overcome; that my team was strong enough to march nonstop to make up that gap; that things could only get better. But I focused on the negative: My invincible Navy SEALs had gotten us lost; my team sponsor, Hi-Tec Sports, could use our failure as an excuse to pull their financial commitment to Eco; and finally, I would become the laughingstock of the entire outdoor industry.

Just then, a Malaysia Airlines turboprop dropped from the sky and landed on the tiny grass strip. Every fiber of my being wanted to jump on that plane and fly home to work on Eco. I would begin damage control immediately. With luck, I could turn this into a victory of some sort.

But I didn't. Team American Pride wasn't going to win, but we needed to finish. We were so lost we didn't know where to go. For me, it was a nightmare as producer of Eco. For the SEALs, the specter of being disgraced in the Special Warfare community loomed. The trouble was none of us had a clue how to get out of Ba Kelalan. I took control of the untenable situation and had a team discussion. We agreed to pay a local guide to show us where that elusive trail was located. We were breaking Raid rules but I didn't care. Forward progress was paramount. Meanwhile, we began squabbling as the strain finally hit us.

Bruce quit two days later from a twisted knee that had swollen to the size of a grapefruit. Now not only were we still in last place and arguing, but we were also officially disqualified. I was very depressed. It couldn't have been worse.

Two days after that, in a bamboo forest somewhere between the fifth and sixth checkpoint, I also decided it was time to go home. It was time to quit.

Now, I feel quitting is the most cowardly of all acts. The American public will forgive many discretions, but not quitting. It'a sign of weakness. Those who quit lack backbone and faith. In a team situation, quitters fail not only themselves, but also teammates who trusted the quitter. I didn't take the act lightly.

I didn't quit right then because I didn't want it to be an impulsive act. After thinking it through completely, I trekked with the team all the way through the harsh hellish jungle section to the beginning of the "fun" river rafting section of the Kubaan River. Wandering down to the river with a bar of soap, I washed myself and decided it was time. I went back and told my teammates. I said something like "I don't need to be kicked in the shins to know it hurts," as a way of reminding them I had already finished twice and had nothing to prove by finishing my third Raid. They tried to talk me out of it, but my mind was made up. I was quitting. I was joining the ranks of those men and women who prefer the easy way out. I rationalized it a hundred different ways in my mind, but the bottom line was that I was still a quitter. Borneo, 1994, was not my finest moment.

But I'm glad it happened.

The path to success is neither straight nor smooth. But the twists and turns and bumps and grooves that make the journey so frustrating also make the destination so rewarding. Truthfully, I didn't deserve to succeed in Borneo. I mean, I'd juggled work, sponsorship raising, and preparation for a whole new race. My training had been minimal. I'd flown halfway around the world in a state of apathy, emotionally distanced myself from my teammates, then seen my dreams of winning the Raid dashed in a maddening 24-hour jungle walkabout, wandering around in last place, then disqualified. If I hadn't quit, chances are I would have begun viewing myself as some sort of Superman. I would have begun thinking I was capable of doing everything in my life half-assed, just to say I'd pulled it off.

Quitting was my wake-up call. I learned three very valuable lessons that propelled my career to the next level.

FOCUS:

It's possible to do a million tasks and accomplish them all. But doing one task expertly is far tougher. I didn't belong in Borneo. My focus should have been preparing to produce Eco-Challenge. Eco was my future and my passion. I was emotionally invested in Eco. Finishing, and hopefully winning, the Raid was a distraction because I'd moved into a new season of my life. I *wanted* to win the Raid, but I *needed* to work on Eco. Nowadays when I get the urge to take on too many tasks, I remember Borneo. I force myself to make hard choices about what I want to do and what I need to do. When I've made my choice I move forward immediately, putting all my energy and focus into what I'm doing.

PERSEVERANCE:

It's easy to quit. In Borneo, it was almost a relief. I could sleep, eat a hot meal, take a hot shower—all those things I couldn't do as a competitor. But that relief was temporary. Within hours of quitting, the comforts weren't so alluring. I missed the hardship of pushing my mental, physical, and emotional limits. I began to wonder, what if? What if I'd pushed on just a little longer? What if I had finished? The end result was that I received more pain by quitting and rationalizing, than if I had simply endured and wandered over the finish line as part of a DQ'ed team.

There is suffering in perseverance, but there is also joy. Borneo taught me to embrace perseverance. When the going gets tough, push on. Life is full of struggles, and if I were to quit every time things got overwhelming I'd be quitting a little every day. So instead of expecting life to be easy, then losing heart when it turns tough, I expect life to challenge me. On those rare occasions when things come easily, I relax and enjoy the moment.

HUMILITY:

When I was standing in the Kubaan, pondering how to tell my teammates I was quitting, a television crew happened to be standing there. Expedition racing is a world without modesty, so I thought nothing of dropping my trousers to continue bathing, even as the camera was turned on and the interviewer began lobbing questions my way. Pants around my ankles, I found myself rationalizing why I was quitting. My words came from the heart. Except for the fact that I was washing my privates as I spoke, my quotes were the sort of footage any good producer would use. The symbolic nature of my interview—literally baring everything—seems poignant in retrospect.

Now, I was shell-shocked about all that had happened. Under normal circumstances I don't give on-camera interviews partially naked. But the potential humiliation felt minor compared with quitting.

That exemplifies best how quitting debases the sense of self—objectivity is gone, replaced by the desire to embrace shame instead of success. That video never made it into race footage, but doubtless it was flashed onto a video monitor, and some editor (or a team of editors) decided whether or not to beam it via satellite back to America. At the very least, several people must have seen this clip. And I don't care. It was false pride that led me to contest the Raid when I wasn't fit. I'd boasted about my team and myself, forgetting that talk is cheap. I deserved to get caught with my pants down.

The day I quit was the day I stopped trying to act cool all the time. I stopped acting like I was better than people. I stopped acting like I could do it all. Those three things are signs of insecurity, anyway. I try to keep my pride hidden and be as polite as possible at all times. People respond better, and more productively, to a humble person than an arrogant one.

The past is the past: When I flew home from Borneo, I wasn't sure whether quitting would negatively affect Eco. I dwelled on it much of the flight, trying to think of clever ways to explain my actions to sponsors and the media. That's when my gut told me not to. Like British Prime Minister Benjamin Disraeli once said, "never complain and never explain." I decided that the past was behind me. I needed to move forward, always forward. Yes, my pride was hurt, and I knew many in the adventure community would disparage me behind my back for quitting. But I couldn't let a minority group of people damage my dream of launching Eco. I would have to endure the wounded pride, the disappointment of not finishing, and the cruel words of those against me. Hurtful things, all, but hardly fatal. If I let them get in the way of Eco, it was nobody's fault but mine.

I remembered a saying I had heard somewhere before, that "when all else fails, the future remains." So before my plane landed in L.A., I'd set Borneo aside. It was over. I got to work on Eco immediately.

I never want to quit anything ever again: Nowadays, people use words like "driven" and "dogmatic" to characterize me. They're right. I've always been like that. But Borneo, 1994, gave that side of my personality a more substantial underpinning.

The failure in Borneo was a blessing in disguise for me. Through failure I gained the strength to make Eco a reality. Through the devastating act of quitting I gained an incentive to persevere, if only so I would never know that awful sensation again. I don't think I would be where I am today if it weren't for those setbacks. Remember: If you're not failing, you're not taking enough chances. Babe Ruth failed 70 percent of the time when he stepped to the plate. And while he's remembered for hitting home runs, it should also be known he was baseball's strikeout king, too. That never stopped him from swinging for the fences.

When failure strikes, take a deep breath, evaluate what went wrong, then push forward again. Always forward.

Choose Teammates Wisely

EVERY GREAT UNDERTAKING is marked by the need for proper teammates. Chosen wisely, teammates will support every goal, no matter how outrageous or seemingly impossible. However, the poorly chosen team makes even the easy quest arduous, and destined to unravel. As I left the Raid behind to focus on making Eco-Challenge the greatest expedition race on the planet, the task felt monumental. But the men and women who came on board to help the cause shared my singular vision—no matter how odd it may have appeared to others—and were committed to making it a reality.

In May 2001, I was flying in a small plane across the equator in Kenya en route to check up on work progress at my new secret location for *Survivor 3* when I looked to my right and saw majestic Mount Kenya. It reminded me of a story about teammates. There once was

an Italian named Felice Benuzzi, who, in 1924, was being held as a prisoner of war in the highlands of central
Kenya. Each day he would gaze out beyond the barbed
wire of the prison compound to the snow-covered
flanks of the highland's focal point, 17,058-foot Mount
Kenya. The mountain took on a mythic place in Benuzzi's mind, a symbol of freedom and dreams and personal triumph. Day by day, the mountain changed
Benuzzi. He began to have crazy, fantastic dreams about
standing atop the mountain. Not after the war, but as
soon as possible. He wasn't a mountain climber. Nor was
he especially fit. In fact, the prison diet had weakened
Benuzzi to the point of malnutrition. But, no matter
what the obstacles, Benuzzi needed to climb that mountain.

He made it his goal to escape from POW Camp 354,
trek to the base of Mount Kenya, and climb to the summit. Then, instead of traveling north to freedom in
Portuguese East Africa (current-day Somalia) to try
and make his way back to Italy, Benuzzi would turn
around, return to the POW camp, and surrender! He
knew full well he could be shot. At the very least
he would be beaten for escaping. The idea was ridicu-
lous, but Benuzzi didn't care. "Have you ever heard of
such madness?" he later wrote, referring to what other
prisoners said about his dream. "To risk catching
a bullet in the ribs for the fun of dying of cold up
there, or of being mauled by wild beasts."

Benuzzi must have been a charismatic fellow, so alive

with passion for his dream that others began to share it. Because when Benuzzi began planning his odyssey, two fellow POWs volunteered to risk all and join him.

What did Benuzzi and his mates expect to receive for climbing the mountain? There were no riches, no publicity, and it certainly wasn't a first ascent. Most men would think the quest foolish. For what Benuzzi craved was the view from the summit—a view he would never forget, even as the guards bludgeoned him and threw him into solitary confinement. Some men might find that intangible unworthy of the risk, but Benuzzi knew that even in the depths of confinement, there is great peace in fulfilling a dream.

Benuzzi and his men began planning. They had no mountaineering experience, no maps, no proper gear or clothing. They stole tins from the mess hall and transformed them into crude crampons. Metal tent stakes were sharpened, attached to broom handles, and became ice axes. Fellow prisoners donated spare items of clothing, which were stitched together to form crude winter clothing.

Benuzzi and his two companions fled the prison and trekked nine days to the foot of Mount Kenya. Under normal conditions it would have taken just three, but their weak physical condition and lack of maps slowed them.

Benuzzi and his comrades worked as a team to select the best route, then pick their way through the rocks and crags to the ring of snow leading to the summit. For

three days they climbed. Then weakness, lack of technical ability, and the illness of one team member forced
them to turn back. Benuzzi was unfazed. He turned his
attention to Point Lenana, Mount Kenya's 16,000-foot
sister peak. Benuzzi and his men began climbing again.
When the same member fell ill again, Benuzzi refused
to turn back a second time. Instead, he built a shelter
for him and pledged to return on the way down.

A day later, Benuzzi stood atop Lenana's summit. I
like to imagine he spied the prison camp so far below,
and felt a sublime wonder at how far his dream had
taken him. He would never have stood there without his
teammates' help.

Benuzzi and his men descended. The triumphant,
sunburned, filthy, famished trio began walking back to
camp. Their gear was left behind in order that they
might travel light. The food ran out four days from the
prison, but they marched on—not toward triumph,
fame, or a hero's welcome, but beatings and captivity.
Sure enough, when they finally arrived, their shocked
captors opened the gates to let them in, then pum-
meled Benuzzi and his mates for escaping.

Those wounds healed, but the glory lived on. Benuzzi
and his fellow climbers spent the rest of their incarcera-
tion awash in the romance of what they had accomplished. "The dream you dream shall live in your
memory," Benuzzi wrote years later, "a delight that will
never stale. It will be your inspiration in years to come."

Eco-Challenge was my Mount Kenya. I was gambling everything I had to climb that mountain. Every penny I'd made from my credit card marketing business had been poured into Eco. I'd mortgaged my house. I had less than $13,000 in the bank—with a young child and by cutting costs at home, it was enough to live on for only a few months. I needed more time than that.

I went to Burt for advice on financing. He told me to persist for another year. If I couldn't pay the bills by then, he'd cover me before my cash ran out. That offer gave me courage and hope, and I was relieved to have the breathing room. Still, I was hardly out of the woods. Regardless of Burt's offer, if Eco failed I would be ruined financially. The thought of selling T-shirts on the beach again felt like a giant step backward. I vowed to do whatever it took to feed my family, and gave Eco my all.

That was my mindset on New Year's Day, 1995. Was I nervous? Yes. Was I scared? Yes!!

But was I excited? Definitely.

Despite my fears, my gut told me the Eco-Challenge would be an enormous success, and that my dream of the Eco-Challenge brand becoming internationally known would come true.

I was Benuzzi, driven by the dream, waiting to savor the delight. I just needed the right team to help me make it come true. I knew I couldn't reach the mountaintop alone.

Beer and Pizza

The Moors have a brilliant proverb describing how to build the optimal team: "Choose your companions before you choose your road."

And that's such a true saying. Teams are a delicate beast. Ideally, each member shares a common goal, whether it be winning a race or completing a project. The selflessness and passion embodied in a group of men and women striving for achievement is wondrous. Positive energy emanates from their labors, breeding high standards and astounding productivity. There is no limit to what a great team can accomplish. They are, in the words of French explorer Pierre Chevalier, like a rope: "together as one man, consisting of the highest human material."

But how to build that great Eco-Challenge management team? Where to find the dynamic individuals willing to work long hours, tilting at windmills? How to motivate them when the inevitable ebb sets in? Human nature can lead to a team's downfall, whether from ego, disinterest, laziness, or the dozens of other daily emotions coursing through disparate individuals.

Eco-Challenge, should it succeed, would be my dream business and, for my employees, a dream job; traveling the world, staging adventure in exotic locales, and living there three months of the year. I just needed the right management team.

That management team came together very quickly

in the form of Brian Terkelson, Lisa Hennessy, Amanda Harrell, and Tricia Middleton. All of them had a few things in common: They were extremely intelligent, they were not afraid of hard work, and they had a passion for adventure. This core group made Eco-Challenge what it is today.

I honestly believe the makings of a great team can be found in one word: chemistry. A group of modestly talented individuals who are team players will accomplish far more than an assortment of geniuses thinking only of themselves. My expedition racing experience taught me that. I can think of no greater test of human dynamics than a team racing in an Eco-Challenge and forced to spend every minute of every day together for two weeks. Every action is communal—eating, sleeping, risking life, even going to the bathroom. The strong teams show their solidarity by stowing their egos in their backpacks, then doing whatever it takes to help each other. They realize that in any long endeavor, weakness and strength become interchangeable—everyone, sooner or later, needs help.

Lesser teams scoff at weakness in others and refuse to admit its presence in themselves. They eventually fracture, bicker, quit. I've noticed that several are so arrogant they don't even learn from their mistakes, and are doomed to repeat them again and again.

There was a moment during the Madagascar Raid that epitomized teamwork for me. After the freefall skydive that began the race, the next stage was two days of arduous trekking through an area known as the Makay Massif. This red-rocked desert is very much like the American Southwest in topography and temperature. Heat waves shimmered off the landscape as we left the drop zone and began the long march through the rugged desert. Skinny longhorn steers known as zebu roamed wild.

We landed our parachutes on a vast plateau, packed them up, and began our trek. One of my teammates, Bruce Schliemann, acting as our advance scout, walked 100 meters ahead, checking for upcoming hazards and keeping a keen eye out for hidden trails that might save a mile or two of walking. Every once in a while Bruce would return to brief us, then range forward again. It was exhausting work, involving a great deal of extra physical and mental energy, but Bruce was eager to do it for the good of the team.

Eight hours into our walk we were in third place, but, as mere fatigue gave way to the harsher realities of dehydration, I began to feel lightheaded. I drank a bit of water and put some food in my body, but otherwise ignored it. Soon my pace flagged. My 30-pound pack ceased to feel lightweight; the pack straps burned into my shoulders and I could have sworn I was carrying a load of anvils. My pace continued to slow and I began falling behind my teammates. The others noticed, but said nothing, hoping I would somehow find the strength to keep up. It was only day one and I believed we would be competitive, but here I was, the team

leader, already trailing my team by a few hundred meters and about to drop.

Bruce hiked back to me. "Give me your pack," he
said.

"No, no. I'm fine," I told him. My pride prevented me
from accepting help.

"It's no big deal. I'll just carry it until you get your
strength back."

"I'm feeling better already. Thanks, but no."

"Mark . . . look. Sometime soon you'll do the same for
me. So just let me carry your pack. We have to reach the
fixed ropes before they close at dark or we'll be stuck
here all night and lose this lead. It's for the good of the
team."

He was right. Getting past the fixed-ropes section
of the course before officials closed it for safety reasons was paramount. I stopped arguing, slipped the
custom-made racing pack from my shoulders, and let
Bruce carry it. I felt guilty at first, as if I literally wasn't
carrying my own weight. But I was grateful for being
able to keep pace with my teammates. My energy returned and we made the cut-off by five minutes, posi-
tioning ourselves firmly in the top five and with other
teams stuck at the ropes until morning. Then the heavens opened up. The searing, dry 100-degree heat was
replaced by a rejuvenating downpour. We climbed the
ropes in the glorious rain and an hour later I was able
to retrieve my pack and pull my own weight again.

I appreciated how Bruce had handled the situation.

He hadn't made a fuss over helping me, made jokes at my expense, or crowed that he was better than me. He'd done what the team needed to advance the team's goals. I was the thankful beneficiary of that kindness and looked forward to returning the favor.

In a strange way, Bruce's act made me stronger. I realized I wasn't alone, nor did I need to shoulder all responsibility for my team. Energy I might have squandered on worry or control could be channeled into racing. But the biggest lesson I learned was never to let pride get in the way of success. Nowadays, when I need help, I ask for it. Not doing so would be silly. Why fail because of pride?

Two days later, after an especially difficult section on a distant plateau where our team had become lost in the 135-degree heat, Bruce climbed down an enormous cliff and scouted for the trail that would show us the way. Finding nothing, he climbed hundreds of feet back up. It was then that the strain of scouting broke Bruce. He was exhausted, delirious, and on the verge of collapse. It was my turn to help. "I'll take your pack," I said to him.

Without a second thought, Bruce handed it over. Instead of taking a prolonged rest while he recovered (or worse, collapsed and had to be airlifted from the course), Team American Pride was able to continue trekking without pause. I learned a lot from Bruce that day.

When I assembled my team for the inaugural Eco-Challenge, I wanted that same selflessness to be our hallmark. But I needed to find a barometer of human character; a way to determine which people would work hard over the long haul, and which were just looking for a paycheck or résumé filler.

I recalled that when I'd trained with Team American Pride, the times when I learned most about my teammates during training—and how I could anticipate their behavior during a race—were at our informal pizza and beer gatherings at Bruce's or Rick's house. Relaxing, eating comfort food, and drinking cold beer acted as a truth serum. I could see which individuals were selfless and caring; ambitious and proud; vain and rude. I planned my relationships with them accordingly. It was through those informal gatherings that we learned to get along and understand each other. I understood my own inadequacies and those of others.

So it was that I devised a caveat to the Moorish proverb, words of wisdom I follow to this day: After choosing my companions, after choosing my road, I always continue to develop friendships within my business team. The Eco management team had a long way to go and I needed to see their true character. By the same token, for our team to be effective, it was also vital that they be aware of my strengths and weaknesses. I have always made it a point to socialize with the staff, especially on location.

Originally, the first member of my team was supposed
to be Gerard Fusil, founder and producer of the Raid.
Because of the staggering size of an expedition race, his
expertise would be crucial. The staging of an expedition race is not unlike a military invasion, with personnel and helicopters and kayaks and whitewater rafts.
There is always a headquarters, complete with a satellite
communications center, video editing bay, motor pool,
field hospital, and media center. Out in the field during
the race, there's search and rescue, coordination of volunteers, transportation of gear . . . the list goes on. Each
location presents a different logistical nightmare, based
on the host country's unique physical and cultural char-
acteristics. As you can imagine, coordinating an expedition race is not as simple as scraping a line on the
ground, shouting "go," watching competitors scurry
into the wilderness, and then hustling to the finish to
see them emerge.

Never having coordinated such an undertaking, I
planned on getting my money's worth of Gerard's field
expertise as I depended on him to answer my myriad of
complex logistical and technical questions. Gerard's
consulting fee was in the six-figure range, but he was the
only person who had successfully pulled off several expedition races, so I gladly paid it.

Soon after, I received crushing news: When Gerard
signed our agreement he was already under contract
with the Raid's parent company, Pub Event. Twenty-five
days before signing with me, he had signed with them to

provide a similar and exclusive service. In fact, their agreement expressly stipulated that he was forbidden to work for any race other than the Raid.

I had been deceived. Not only was there no way of retrieving my money (short of flying to Paris and filing suit), but with Gerard out of the picture I was faced with the brutal realization that I was now the technical and logistical mastermind behind Eco-Challenge. It was like a linebacker being sent into the Super Bowl without a playbook.

Problem was, I'm not a linebacker. I'm a quarterback—a leader. My strengths lie in creativity, production, and coordination. But, as I said earlier, when it comes time to seek extreme success, I'll do any and every task necessary to see a goal completed.

I was scared, as I felt that I didn't even know what I didn't know. Gerard had been like a security blanket and had provided courage. Now I was alone.

I took a deep breath, thought through the hundreds of logistical riddles and technical obstacles looming before me, and found the resolve to go forward. I was capable of learning it all as we went along. It wouldn't be pretty, but the abrupt learning curve was definitely the sort of sink or swim scenario in which I thrive.

I could not, however, do it alone. What I needed was someone smart to share ideas and strategize with. I had the vision but not the formal training. For that task I brought in Brian Terkelsen, an investment banker from New York who had abandoned Wall Street to make a living at adventure out west. We talked over pizza and beer. I saw that he was not only brilliant and driven, but that he truly saw the enormous financial possibilities of the adventure market. He had done his homework. Brian informed me of research showing that family travel adventures such as white-water rafting on the Snake River and mountain biking atop the slick red-rock trails outside Moab were becoming enormously popular even as hotel rooms in traditional travel destinations like Waikiki were going begging. Americans were falling in love with stepping outside the comfort zone. Brian helped me confirm that my gut feeling was right. This new trend was a lifestyle shift instead of a short-term travel phenomenon. Better yet, we were among the first to capitalize upon it.

Brian became my fellow climber on our personal Mount Kenya, using his buttoned-down corporate-speak to complement my drive, vision, and passion. With him as a teammate, I was able to chart the long-term future of the Eco-Challenge, even when those words represented just a dream.

Brian's first act after joining my team was crunching numbers to check the viability of, and design a five-year plan for the new Eco-Challenge Lifestyles corporation. He forecast earnings based on the several different indicators that might prove my hunch about America falling in love with adventure. To my relief, we were right. The dollars were out there. We just had to go and get them.

Know Your Teammates' Limitations

The ordeal began in earnest in early 1994. From the creative vision already in my head I could see that the three greatest obstacles to a successful Eco-Challenge were, in no particular order: 1. obtaining a proper location; 2. obtaining the necessary permits; and, 3. raising the money to fund Eco-Challenge.

Brian and I tackled the most logical, and easily solved, dilemma first: location. Ideally it would be Alaska. More than any other state, that vast state defines wilderness. Mountains, ice, grizzly bears, and wild rivers—perfect. Other than cold and the daunting cost of shipping tons of supplies and vital personnel so far north, there could be no better location.

Then Brian worked the numbers and showed me two things: Alaska was expensive; and Eco would serve as a tremendous tourism vehicle for the host state. Through television and the print media, scenic images from Eco would provide millions of impressions. Not only would it be a race, but also a massive tourism commercial for the lucky state. Based upon Alaska's costs and seeming reluctance to help us out financially, it made sense to look elsewhere before committing North. It was our hope that interested states would offer governmental support with permits and legalities and maybe even provide some financial incentives to ease our tight budgetary burdens. We mailed detailed proposals to the tourism bureaus of several different states.

I knew we wanted to have Eco-Challenge somewhere in the West. Not only is there a lack of population density and an abundance of wide-open spaces, but thanks to the "Hollywood Western," that region embodies adventure to the world. What other corner of the globe can claim its own film genre?

In addition to my early talks with Alaska, I now had discussions with officials in Montana, Wyoming, and Utah. Each of these states offered thousands of miles of rugged wilderness, white-water rivers, and dramatic mountains. All were symbols of the American West, and would have resonated in viewers' minds as being worthy of hosting "the toughest race on earth." The sweep and grandeur of their landscapes made location scouting seem more like a primer on appreciating America's beauty than real work. I could have chosen any of them and had a dynamic event.

But I chose Utah.

The deciding factor was participation by the governor. He allowed me the use of his private plane for my initial survey to fly all over the state, seeing with my own eyes the canyons and rivers and deserts so perfect for Eco-Challenge. Beyond that, he made it clear that hosting Eco-Challenge was a priority. This unexpected wooing carried tremendous heft. Having the governor as an ally was vital, because his participation would smooth the permit process. We needed those approvals for the use of public lands in order to trek the deserts, raft pristine canyons, and even fly helicopters during

Eco. Obtaining them was a notoriously tedious and expensive undertaking. Without proper help, the permitting process could drag on for years—years that we
didn't have—or stop the race altogether if permits
were denied. In choosing Utah, I had enlisted the governor as a powerful new member of the Eco-Challenge
team.

I spent a month studying maps and flying low over
Utah, deciding where to put the course. In a state that
diverse and vast, the choice was not easy. If I went with a
more alpine race, the Uinta Mountains near the
Wyoming border made sense. For canyons, the whole
southeastern corner of the state was one giant maze of
cliffs, gorges, and narrow slot canyons. For a pure desert
gruelathon, I could send teams through the Great Salt
Lake Desert, along the Nevada border.

In the end, I chose a route honoring Grand Canyon
explorer John Wesley Powell's journey of a century before. Starting just south of the snow-capped Uintas, the
route would loosely parallel the languid Green River as
it made its way toward the Colorado River. The finish,
fittingly, would be a 70-mile kayak paddle from the roil-
ing Colorado into the placid water of Lake Powell. I envisioned fireworks announcing the winner, and a gala
post-race party under the stars.

I hired a series of guides (white-water, climbing, etc.)
to set the course. Then I personally trekked, climbed,
mountain biked, rafted, and canoed parts of each section. The beauty and isolation was stunning, and it was

impossible to believe that the neon and glitz of Las Vegas were just a few hundred miles over the desert horizon.

America is a marvelous country, and her cities can feel so crowded that it seems the entire nation is a dense mass of humanity. But in the desert of eastern Utah, hearing no sound but my footfalls or the roar of the wind, marveling at land untouched by development or roads, appearing just as it did when time began, I knew the peace only solitude and communion with nature can bring. More than ever, I knew my race must be there.

Course maps in hand, I strode into the State Tourism department a few days later, expecting to march back out with a satchel of permits. "This course looks great," they enthused. "Fantastic."

"Thanks," I said. "Can I pick up those permits now?"

They looked at me as if I were slow. "Permits?"

"Yes. To get access to that land for the race."

"Permits?"

"That's right."

There was an embarrassed silence. "Oh, no. We don't handle permits here. All that land you've chosen? That's federal land. We can't give permits for federal land."

So much for having the governor on my side. What followed was a six-month, quarter-million-dollar wrangle with the Bureau of Land Management. Precious sponsorship dollars I'd accrued to cover race expenses went into hiring consultants to perform environmental impact reports. The free permits I'd expected became very expensive. Then environmental groups noted that bighorn sheep and peregrine falcons lived on the course. My April race date conflicted with the mating of the sheep and hatching of falcon nestlings. The environmentalists feared my athletes would disturb them.

It was bad enough having to battle the Bureau of Land Management, but the irony of environmentalists opposing my race was surreal. My Eco-Challenge was designed to heighten public awareness of the earth, not destroy it. The land we were traveling through was used year-round by ranchers to graze cattle and was open to four-wheel-drive vehicles. I couldn't understand how a few hundred people passing through in small 5-person groups on foot over a week-long period could be any more disruptive than thousands of cattle eating and sleeping and defecating there on a daily basis. Not to mention the route I'd chosen was 90 percent on 4WD tracks that were used regularly by off-road vehicles. The Eco-Challenge standards for leaving land as we found it were so stringent that it was a mandatory requirement for teams to carry out all trash—including bodily waste—or face disqualification. Not so much as an energy bar wrapper would be left behind.

Clearly, we weren't going to cause an impact, and would promote eco-tourism. But Eco-Challenge was a lightning rod for attack because we had the backing of the governor and the national prominence from MTV. Environmental groups chose to focus on us instead of a coal plant being built in the same region. Despite it being a far bigger environmental concern, attacking a coal plant isn't sexy, and doesn't draw big media.

Would Eco-Challenge lead to an increase in eco-tourism in Utah? Definitely. And that was the crux of the discussion. The various wilderness alliances saw land use as a bad thing. In some ways I could see their point. Ongoing use of the land would be harmful. However, I believed the benefits outweighed the negatives. With responsible and regular usage by the public comes a sense of propriety and desire to protect. In the long run, that land is less likely to be developed because people have had a chance to appreciate its beauty and will fight to protect it.

On the opposite side of the argument, Utah's cattle ranchers also fought against Eco-Challenge. They saw the word "Eco" in the title, read about MTV's involvement, and lumped us with those environmentalists who have decided cattle are bad for the land and must be banished entirely. However, I totally disagreed with the hardcore environmentalists who forgot that many of the ranchers were from the same families that had done the hard physical work of taming the west a century before. Some of the fringe environmental groups were even sniping at cattle with guns and threatening to do the same to Eco-Challenge athletes!

I had unwittingly walked into the firestorm that defines land usage in the modern American West. I had added a new sort of fuel to the fire and had no friends on either side.

The lesson learned was about education. I hadn't studied the powers of the governor's office, nor studied which agency owned the lands on which I wanted to race, nor read up on the land wars between ranchers and environmentalists. Would I have still had my race in Utah? Undoubtedly, despite the permitting headaches, and environmental bother. I liked that Utah's diverse, primitive terrain was a stark reminder of how small mankind is in the big scheme of things. I could hardly blame the governor for my political naiveté.

But I still wish I had known that my most politically connected teammate, the governor, had no power over the lands I needed. Never again would I enter into a team relationship without learning exactly what my new ally could and could not offer.

As for the permits? The process dragged on for months, and became a bureaucratic nightmare.

RAISING MONEY FOR ECO-CHALLENGE proved a different sort of hurdle. Our budget was one million dollars, a figure we hoped to achieve through sponsorships, entry fees, and the sale of television rights (which went to MTV). At the same time that I was designing the course and fighting to secure permits, I was also working the phones and flying about the country to wrangle financing. I didn't see the Eco-Challenge as just a race, but as a lifestyle brand that applied to all men and women, so I didn't limit my search to corporations aligned with the outdoor industry. Other than alcohol and tobacco, I felt every product had a place with my competition. I pitched Eco-Challenge to companies ranging from airlines to auto manufacturers to soft drink bottlers, assuring them that my offbeat event would someday be the standard by which all endurance competitions—and adventure itself—would be measured.

It helped that the athletes already believed in what I was doing. Thanks to my "audacious" ad in *Triathlete*, I had no shortage of eager squads. The 50-team limit was met a month before race day.

However, few corporations saw my vision and came on board with the sort of massive financial commitment I needed. I needed seven-figure deals and was getting high-five and low-six. The money to meet budget requirements was accumulating, but slowly. Just as with the permits, there would be no race if I couldn't procure enough backing. I worked 18 hours a day during the first five months of 1995, half of that time with a phone pressed to my ear. I tried to remain calm, but the pressure was enormous.

It was then that The Easy Way Out tempted me. A large company called with an offer that would put an end to my woes. For $500,000 they wanted to buy the race sponsorship, substituting their company's name for the word *Eco* in the race title. They were happy to be associated with the adventure aspect of my race but didn't believe the ecology part would hold long-term value. How wrong they were. In addition, they would own the event, the name, the rights—everything. I would walk away with a half-million dollars free and clear, but still have the headaches of producing the XYZ Challenge. The alternate side of that was that if I turned down the offer, and Eco didn't happen for lack of financing and permits, I would be left with nothing. Hello, London.

I couldn't take their money.

It sounds crass to use this term, but I knew I had come to a time in my life where having balls counted for everything. That company wouldn't have shown interest unless they saw the same enormous potential in Eco-Challenge that I did. If they were willing to spend money, so were others. Yes, I was out of money, depending on cash advances from credit cards to pay the mortgage. But taking The Easy Way Out would undermine the purity of my Eco quest and cheapen my future dreams. The clock was ticking, and the money was rolling in slowly. I would just have to work harder.

And I did. Amazingly, my proposals found their way into the proper hands, and several lucrative deals ensued, most notably with Hi-Tec Sports and JanSport. Once we reached the one-million-dollar benchmark I was free to focus my energies on securing permits. My relief was enormous.

Then a week before the race was to begin, as competitors had already begun arriving in Utah to acclimate to local conditions, Brian came to me with bad news. There was, he told me, "a mistake" in our budget numbers. "How big a mistake?" I asked, not sure I wanted to hear the answer.

"A half-million dollars."

I sagged. In reality, when it comes to budget deficits, I've always found it's practical to double any figure. So I was looking at a million-dollar shortfall, just one week before the start of the most pivotal event in my professional life. Where in the world was I going to find a million dollars?

I had a huge problem, but I had learned that huge problems tend to make me calm and focused. I would find an answer. Combing the list of corporations we'd sent sponsorship packets to, we noted that several had the financial wherewithal to pay us a million dollars within the next seven days. I made hundreds of calls, narrowing the list down further, weeding out those corporations who would not act quickly. The list was still too long, and time was running out. I needed to make a decision about which company we would pinpoint. It was all or nothing. No time for anything else.

I had a gut feeling about MET-Rx, the dietary supplement company. They were young, aggressive, and eager to crack the competitive energy bar market. They also had loads of capital. I arranged a meeting, and pitched Eco-Challenge with an enthusiasm (and desperation) I'd never known. MET-Rx was dazzled, and agreed to come on board as race sponsor for $650,000. The race would go off with a deficit, but it would go off.

So here we were, almost financed, with less than a

week until the race started. Onsite, fifty teams, MTV, *Dateline NBC, Good Morning America,* forty journalists, and hundreds of volunteers had arrived in Utah, expecting a race. All that was missing, at this very last stage, were the permits. Everyone would have had to turn around and go home (though not without putting a price on my head) if those damn permits weren't approved.

I must have had an intuition about it all because I felt incredibly calm throughout those last few crazy days. My "gut" was right again because finally, on April 21, 1995, four days before the start of the first Eco-Challenge, the final permits got approval. The race was a go. My vision was about to be realized.

Be Aware of How You Communicate

When I think back on the wonder and calamity of that first race, a series of images cross my mind: the start at sunrise, with teams galloping across the desert on horseback while ABC's *Good Morning America* broadcasts live from our location; the canyoneering section, where the narrow chasms were often filled with rivers fed by snowmelt; courageous competitors, realizing that swimming the frigid waters was the only means of forward progress, boldly tackling the challenge; Horseshoe Canyon, where teams rappelled. I can still see how ant-like they appeared against those massive Biblical cliffs.

And the finish on Lake Powell, with flares shot into the sky to celebrate the arrival of the victorious French squad, Hewlett-Packard (whose corporate sponsor showed considerable vision by subsidizing a team whose impact wandered far beyond H-P's core business unit). Only 42 percent of all teams finished, which proved how tough my race was.

But most of all, I remember Team Operation Smile, and a wonderful 72-year-old woman named Helen Klein. The team's goal was to raise money for an international organization whose corps of doctors traveled to Third World countries performing surgery to repair cleft palates in children. That simple procedure, so common in America, is almost unheard of in developing nations.

The basic premise behind an Eco-Challenge is that a team of explorers is navigating unknown countryside. They must navigate from Point A to Point B (start to finish) with map and compass. Travel is always done through non-motorized means of locomotion. Each team must be coed, because I feel that too few sports provide full equality to women. In Eco-Challenge, the mountains, rivers, and forest are equal-opportunity punishers.

When a race location is announced, teams are told which disciplines to train for, but are not given course maps, the order of events, or even the distances. Teams travel from checkpoint to checkpoint in a nonstop journey, the speed of which is determined by the teams themselves (some race quickly while others tour the course, taking in the scenery). Teams are given a beacon to activate in event of emergency, but otherwise no outside assistance of any kind is allowed.

Team Operation Smile had a roster of true adventurers—a few were from Europe, a few from America. All, with the exception of Helen, were in their thirties and forties. Helen was their senior by a number of years. She had come to exercise late in life, taking up running as a means of staying fit in her forties. Within a decade she was completing marathons and ultra-marathons. Eventually, she and her husband put on a race of their own, the Western States, a 100-mile trail race in Northern California's Sierra Nevada Mountains. Helen not only coordinated the competition, she completed the entire course several times.

Despite this endurance racing background, Helen looked old and frail compared to the U.S. Marines and twenty-something triathletes populating that first Eco. She got more than a few odd looks. Only Team Operation Smile saw the potential greatness in this tough great-grandmother.

Helen and her teammates' goal was to finish, not to win. So they raced slowly. They worked together, helping and encouraging each other. During the mountain bike portion, Helen somehow managed to fall off her bike on a flat section of ground. Without reason, she just fell. None of her teammates moaned or rolled her eyes or gave her a hard time in any way. None of them had that strained look on their faces that translated into "We shouldn't have brought this old lady along." Instead, they stitched up the open cut above her eye, helped her back on her bike, said a few encouraging words, and got on their way again. They genuinely cared for her.

Their actions showed Team Operation Smile was cognizant that *how* teammates communicate means more than communication itself, and that unspoken communication can be more powerful than words.

I think because of technology and the use of e-mail as a means of communication, many of us have lost touch with the nuances of the spoken word or even a subtle look. We've become a bit impersonal. But Eco-Challenge is always face-to-face, and so I have seen the effects of improper communication, especially of the unspoken variety.

We only have so much energy within us. That energy has to get us through each day, whether it be at work or on the Eco-Challenge course. But every time we have a negative encounter with another human being, that energy gets drained. Human problems drain energy like nothing else. I think of it like a bathtub of water. Just as the bathtub is full of water, so the Eco-Challenge athlete begins the race with a full supply of energy. The bathtub is full; there's ten days to race. You can't put any water back in the bathtub because you only have a certain amount of energy to last the race. The moment you start the race, the plug is pulled ever so slightly from the drain. Ideally, only 10 percent of that water (energy) drains from an athlete each day. If the athlete paces him- or herself well and is a fair and compassionate human being, always focusing on the team's goals, he or she will reach the finish line ten days later just as the last bit of water empties down the drain.

But when communication goes awry, energy is drained from the bathtub at five to six times the rate it should. The team is yanking the plug from the drain, instead of peeling it back just a crack. Like when a team member berates another, saying they should have trained harder, they're not fit enough, or they're letting the team down—all of which is completely pointless—it's obvious that person is going to feel much, much worse for being yelled at. If someone's feeling bad, it's much harder to carry their pack. I'll never forget the team that was screaming at one another, pointing fingers of blame for this mistake or that mistake. Of course, that sort of thing happens all the time at Eco. But what made that particular team special was their name: Faultless.

Energy can also be drained through unspoken communication of the negative variety: the dirty look, the deliberate bump, and worst of all, faking compassion—saying to some poor guy, "don't worry, I'll carry your pack, you just carry yourself," but doing it not out of compassion, but in a condescending way that makes the person feel terrible. Those insidious forms of poor communication are what destroy teams. Anger festers inside both parties.

In these cases, the bathtub empties rapidly, all remaining energy is lost, and the team fails.

I think energy loss through poor communications was why a very fit team that included some U.S. Marines didn't finish the 1995 Eco-Challenge, but Team Operation Smile with its little old lady did. True, they finished in last place. But they finished. They achieved their goal. Team Operation Smile showed one of the true secrets of Eco-Challenge: It's not just about the fitness and the skill, it's also about the energy retained through positive, honest human communication.

Team Operation Smile conserved their energy by avoiding negative communication. They never entirely pulled the plug from the drain. When they did communicate, it was in a positive, reinforcing manner. They didn't blame one another when things went wrong. They were humble and flexible. If a problem arose, such as getting lost, Team Operation Smile never bickered. Instead, they'd look at the situation, and say, "We're in this together, let's deal with this."

Helen was a smart, tough lady. Once, when she and her teammates had run out of water, they came across a puddle in the desert. Another team was already there, staring at a dead cow lying in the water, wondering whether or not the water was safe to drink. Helen didn't hesitate, and got down on her knees to begin drinking. "It's drink or die, sweetie," she said. "It's fifty miles to the next water and you'll never make it without drinking now. If you get sick, it'll be after the race and that's okay." But it was probably more to the credit of her teammates that Team Operation Smile finished. They didn't complain, they supported one another the whole way, and they had their egos in their backpacks.

I realized, after watching Helen's team paddle across the finish line on Lake Powell, that having her on the team was actually a gift for Team Operation Smile. Women in general—and an older woman like Helen, specifically—are actually better in the Eco-Challenge than men. They're willing to give and receive help without attitude. Men are scared to ask for help, as they think it will make them look weak. But it doesn't matter to women. They're just smart. They'll size up a situation, and admit they can't conquer it alone, then immediately ask for help. Or they will say, "I can't carry this pack, do me a favor, carry the pack for me over this hill because you look strong." Can you imagine a guy saying that? A guy would rather die. In most cases, though not all, when a guy's exhausted, he's not thinking about the team's goals, he's thinking about looking good. He would never admit being in trouble, let alone hand his pack to some five-foot-tall woman who happens to be stronger.

You know what? On good teams, men and women don't worry about how they look as individuals. They worry about the team. The person in trouble is not a man or a woman, but a teammate.

The greatest lesson I learned at that first Eco was how ordinary people on a good team can achieve extraordinary things. But a highly skilled team that has focus, knows how to communicate, and that really cares for one another as a team is unbeatable. The group I've got working for me now—producers, cameramen, sound engineers, editors, assistants, course designers, mountain guides—is just such a team. We've stood by one another through thick and thin, driven by loyalty and focus on the goal. They are the very best.

I'm reminded of a quote by oil billionaire J. Paul Getty: "Take away the oil fields and the factories, but leave me my fifty best people and I'll have it all back double in five years."

AFTER UTAH, I FLEW HOME to Southern California, hoping for several weeks of much-needed rest. I didn't get it. ESPN was already calling, wanting me to set up an Eco-Challenge at the X Games. Two great things came from that event: First, my fee retired the Utah debts once and for all, putting Eco-Challenge Lifestyle into the black (it's been there ever since). Second, we had a chance to immediately produce another Eco-Challenge, putting into practice all we had learned in Utah. The X-Games Eco-Challenge went very well and helped my Eco-Challenge Production team gain and keep the enormous confidence they still exhibit today.

When MTV balked at airing another Eco-Challenge without a stipulation that all competitors be between 18 and 25, I secured meetings with ABC, FOX, NBC, and

CBS to pitch Eco. Though all of them turned me down, my relationship with the Big Four networks had begun.

It was an exciting and frightening time in my life. And though I could have been content to stay in Los Angeles and develop other projects, adventure called to me. I needed to be in the bush. There I find solitude and beauty and purity and focus. That's where my heart lies. As head of the Eco-Challenge team, I had an obligation to my teammates not to lose that focus by getting caught up in the bright lights of Hollywood. I realized that once the "method producer" became just another guy sitting behind a desk, taking meetings instead of trekking the course and rafting the white water, I ceased to be the man I wanted to be.

So it was that I began planning the 1996 Eco-Challenge. My goal was to take it beyond the American borders. I wanted the race to have a more international feel. I was thinking that British Columbia would be ideal.

That was a heady time. And the number of obstacles my team and I had hurdled to make the Eco-Challenge dream come true were forgotten as the rosy glow of success surrounded us.

Never underestimate what a great team can accomplish.

Perseverance Produces Character
(and Character Produces Hope)

THERE IS A FALLACY inherent in achieving a goal—that when the moment of achievement finally arrives, life gets easy. Everything is calm. It's a fallacy that says it's easier when the battle is won, let's relax, we have achieved our goal. Let's stop trying so hard.

That is complete and utter nonsense. First off, success is addictive, and begets more success. The first thing I do after completing a goal is set another. It would be a waste of all I learned and endured to not take that bold step upward to the next level of personal achievement. Second, life is about conflict. When I achieve a goal, I realize that conflict comes with the territory. I step up to the plate and meet those challenges head-on. Like the old saying goes, "When the going gets tough, the tough get going." And the going always—inevitably—gets tough. So be ready for those moments and confront them until the challenge is handled. Each of them will make you stronger and more self-confident, so instead of bemoaning challenge, be glad it found you.

That was my mindset after finally getting Eco off the ground. I had achieved success, I had completed the first part of my Eco-Challenge goal, and I knew that a slew of roadblocks would present themselves on the journey to the second half of that goal. Step One had been to produce an Eco-Challenge. I'd now produced two. The next step was to make Eco-Challenge the premier expedition race on the planet, usurping all other races, including the Raid. The way to do this, I knew, was through better television. I began an active search for a network that would allow me to produce the sort of epic Eco-Challenge television show I had in mind. Through proper production and distribution, the medium of television would make *Eco-Challenge* and *adventure* synonymous.

I'm not frightened of competition, because it can only make you better. Strangely, competition has taken on negative connotations in the past decade or so. The implied aggressiveness scares some people, and has made competition politically incorrect. Well, you know what? Life is competition. And the Eco-Challenge, as the perfect blend of sport, human dynamics, and adventure, is the epitome of competition. Athletes race against other teams, against nature, against the environment, and against their bodies. Whether competing in the Eco-Challenge, vying for a CEO's position, or racing for that last spot in a crowded mall parking lot, everyone on earth competes.

Denying an attraction to competition, I think, is a form of fear. It's like procrastination or rationalization. People often feel that they need to be 100 percent sure they'll succeed before starting something difficult. What they're really saying is they're afraid to compete and fail. But really, are there any sure things in life? Are you ever 100 percent sure it's the right time to start a business, change jobs, get married? Of course not. One can never be sure. My philosophy is that I'll jump in and commit even if I'm only *40 percent* or *50 percent* sure it will succeed. Mike Sears, who served as director on the first Eco-Challenge, was quoted once as saying: "Burnett is the kind of person who would walk down Fifth Avenue in New York, saying 'Come on everybody, let's follow the parade,' even when there's no parade. But within a couple blocks people follow him to the parade, and he'll be leading it. I can't decide whether he's courageous or crazy."

I'm probably a little of both. But there's no denying that the pressure of competition sharpens me, pushes me, makes demands of me. Instead of denying the attraction, I prefer to embrace it. In competition, as in failure, are sown the seeds of success.

Don't Make Excuses

In January of 1996 a friend of mine, Tom Werthheimer, arranged a meeting between myself and Greg Moyer, president of Discovery Channel. Moyer was looking for fresh programming with a global scope. Discovery Channel International had already expanded and was in over 100 countries and needed the programming to give themselves a genuine worldwide brand. What he saw in Eco was an adventure Olympics. We ended up marrying Discovery Channel and Eco-Challenge over a cup of coffee at the National Association of Television Executive Producers' Conference in Las Vegas. The deal, signed on a scrap of paper with numerous hand-written changes, gave Discovery Channel global multi-media rights in exchange for a production fee and a rights fee. Our first race together would take place in August 1996, in British Columbia.

The challenge for me would be personal and professional. On the professional level, attempting to narrow hundreds of hours of footage into five hours for broadcast would be daunting. That our deadline was just ten weeks after the race would end made it all the more demanding. More than ever before, I would need to focus on my duties as executive producer and choose the right teammates as I expanded.

Personally, I had never worked within a corporate structure. My company is not like other companies. We don't dress in suits and ties. The staff is small. The atmosphere is collegiate, yet workaholic. Instead of glitzy office space, we reside in a nondescript building. With the amount of time I spend on location, and the fact that we rarely have visitors that we need to impress (only our shows can do that) fancy office space is a waste.

Discovery, on the other hand, was a large and powerful international cable network—a 7-billion-dollar corporation with thousands of employees. Their size dictated a hierarchy, complete with mid-level managers and high-powered executives. I wasn't daunted by the structure, because the trade-off was Discovery's reputation for quality television and their ability to put Eco in 140 million households in 130 countries.

I worked hard in the months leading up to British Columbia. To ensure that the production would go smoothly, I promoted a young coordinator named Lisa Hennessy to producer. She had performed impeccably in Utah and at the X Games. As Eco-Challenge producer, she proved to have enormous bandwidth, nerves of steel, and good financial management. To ensure that the course would challenge competitors far more than Utah, I enrolled a highly respected senior mountain guide named Scott Flavelle to set the route. He did a masterful job. Both Lisa and Scott have remained with Eco-Challenge and Lisa is now my co-executive producer, literally running the company.

Scott's race route would begin an hour north of Whistler, along the banks of the crystal-clear Lillooett River. Whereas navigation in Utah was as simple as setting a line toward the horizon and trekking toward it, in British Columbia I was sending teams straight up and down forest-shrouded mountain after forest-shrouded mountain. The pines and alder grew as dense as trees in a rain forest. Except for atop summits or along rivers, competitors would be unable to see the horizon.

British Columbia's forests hid many black bears and grizzly bears. The key to passing through the forest safely was in not surprising the bears, so I required every competitor to wear small bells that rang with every step. (The locals began telling a joke: How can you tell black bear scat from grizzly scat? Black bear scat is filled with berries and grizzly scat is filled with bear bells.) Less dangerous, but far more annoying, were the omnipresent swarms of fat mosquitoes and a nefarious plant known as devil's club. The club's leaves were smooth and fern-like on top, but the bottoms were coated with needle-like thorns that embedded themselves in human skin when grabbed. Above all, the worst annoyance in British Columbia was a plant known as slide alder. This thick tangle of leaves and branches sprouted in the swaths of forest cleared by avalanche, growing over and around the thick trunks of toppled trees. It was pure hell through which to trek. I came to think of this horticultural snare as nature's "No Trespassing" sign.

All in all, however, it was a perfect patch of wilderness in which to hold an Eco-Challenge. Majestic but grueling.

I desperately wanted to impress the people at Discovery Channel, to show them we deserved to be on the same team. We brought sixteen camera crews—twice as many as we'd used for MTV. I liked the increased size of

than the Raid or any other race. On the professional side, the February 1997 broadcast on Discovery was a ratings success, for which I received my first Emmy nomination.

Be a Samurai

More than anything, Eco-Challenge has taught me about the courage of the human spirit. As I write this, there have been seven Eco-Challenges, on five continents. I have watched in fascination as men and women from over 50 countries have willingly subjected themselves to my race. They harden their bodies and minds through months of running, mountain biking, weight lifting, and kayaking, hoping that their preparation will be sufficient for whatever obstacles are thrown at them by my course and Mother Nature. As I've mentioned, I don't give away course details prior to the pre-race briefing on the eve of competition, so these people truly know they must be prepared for anything.

Eco-Challenge is a metaphor for life, where men and women are thrown together and told to get along every minute of every day, despite being cold, tired, wet, hungry, and miserable. The brave souls contesting my race endure the mountains and rivers and jungles gladly. Normal people, under normal conditions, know better than to venture outside in weather my teams must endure. I'm proud to say that Eco-Challenge expedition racers accept it as part of the game, and never complain about the hardship. In fact, they embrace the hardship. And that—more than nature, being on television, or physical fitness—is why people race Eco-Challenge. For they know that hardship is the only way they can find out what they're truly made of—whether they'll back off when the going gets tough, or whether they'll find the courage to be bold, and become their own hero in the process. It doesn't matter whether they win or lose, but how they play the game. I find the purity of that notion inspiring.

One thing that never fails to amaze me is the ingenuity of the human spirit. How, when a team or individual wants something badly enough, they'll scour their brain for a solution to even the most daunting problem rather than quit. I'm reminded of the Japanese team East Wind at the Queensland, Australia, race in 1997. Team East Wind had come to Australia to win, talking openly about their samurai spirit, and how this bold warrior mentality would drive them to victory. The samurai spirit was that of a warrior: Inner strength was paramount, failure was not an option, every problem had a solution, and the body was a pliable tool, disciplined and controlled by the mind. Little did Team East Wind know that they would come to exemplify samurai spirit in the most amazing way—but through defeat, not victory.

The race began on foot near the lava tubes of Undara, in the grassy heat of the Australian Outback, then they canoed along the Herbert River to a ropes section at the Herbert River Falls. Teams would enter the rain forest halfway through the race, then trek up and over Mount Bartle Frere, at a mile high the highest point in Queensland. Finally, after descending Bartle Frere, they would trek to the ocean, then kayak north along the Great Barrier Reef to the finish in Cairns.

In the afternoon of the race's seventh day, the victorious Team Eco-Internet paddled across the finish line in Cairns. Champagne and congratulatory hugs were in abundance. Then I received word by walkie-talkie of a far more dire situation back out on the course. Team East Wind was back at the 24th checkpoint, about to climb Mount Bartle Frere. Problem was, Nihoko Hayama, their lone female member, had suffered a severe injury to her Achilles tendon during the preceding 65-kilometer mountain biking stage. She could walk, but just barely, and only on flat ground. Walking uphill, because of her Achilles injury, was out of the question.

The medical crew at PC 24 examined Hayama, then gave Team East Wind the bad news: They would have to quit the race. There was no way she would be able to climb Bartle Frere. It was an awesome mountain, covered with thick jungle and sharp boulders, and so rugged that a lone climber had disappeared there the previous summer. Ostrich-sized birds known as cassowaries, with huge claws like raptors, were known to attack people. There were leeches and poisonous snakes everywhere. Because it's so intimidating, the aborigines believe the mountain is sacred, and that their spirits protect it.

Most of all, Bartle Frere was an awful mountain to climb. When I'd trekked the course before the race with my mountain guides, I'd found Barlte Frere spooky and very hard. Given Hayama's condition, there was no way Team East Wind could go on. The Australian medical crew felt very bad about breaking the news.

To everyone's surprise, East Wind's team captain, Atsushi Suzuki, convinced them that the team wasn't ready to quit. They had come to Australia with the goal of completing the Eco-Challenge, and they meant to accomplish that goal. He spoke to the medical team in halting English. "If she cannot walk, we will carry her."

The doctors were incredulous. "You'll do what, mate?"

"We will carry her."

The medical team taped Hayama's ankle tightly. She was able to bike the 35 miles to the base of the mountain, then she trekked the few miles of gentle slopes leading to the almost-vertical jungle trail. It was then that her three teammates (beginning with the Australia race, each team featured four members instead of five) took turns carrying her up the mountain. "Everyone," Suzuki said of the decision to go on, "has to come to terms with what the Eco-Challenge offers them."

Bertle Frere begins at sea level, and climbs abruptly to almost a mile high, so it's a very steep slope. Hayama fell hard several times, one time slipping off a teammate's back into a pile of jagged, algae-covered rocks. Her teammates, deprived of their natural balance and burdened with a woman weighing over 100 pounds, took slow, awkward steps. When I watched the footage of them tenaciously clambering over fallen trees and rocky outcroppings, I sat there in amazement at their fortitude. "Carrying her to the summit became our competition," Suzuki noted. "We have a saying in Japan, that once you fall, you are closer to death, but not yet dead. We tapped into our Japanese spirit to carry her up the mountain. That was our challenge."

For ten long hours, Team East Wind picked their way up Bartle Frere, step by laborious step. Now and again they would appear in a clearing and feel the sun on their faces, but otherwise the trek was accomplished in the overcast dank rain forest. The summit was wreathed in clouds, so when Team East Wind stepped from the jungle into the checkpoint, it was as if they were mystical apparitions. Finally, they put Hayama down and rested. They had completed their goal. They had shown Samurai spirit, and risen to the challenge.

Rarely have I seen that kind of spirit. When people are as far back in the pack as East Wind, they have a hard time finding a reason to take another step. Their fantastic dreams about the glory of simply finishing have been forgotten, beaten out of them by hardship, exhaustion, and suffering. Not only did Team East Wind find a reason to take that next step, but they did so after being given a very palatable reason for quitting. They could have gone home and nobody would have blamed them for failing. Injury is a fact of life.

But Team East Wind had a goal of finishing the Eco-Challenge. They never lost sight of that. They even made a challenge of climbing the mountain—made it a goal—which I'm sure made it more motivating when the going got tough.

Sadly, Team East Wind never crossed the finish line at that Eco-Challenge. Their spirited ascent of Mount Bartle Frere took such a long time that they missed a mandatory time cut-off. I think, however, that Team East Wind's perseverance showed the depth of their character. If each member of the team uses that same perseverance in every aspect of their life—marriage, business, fitness, education, and so on—they will always be a success.

When life gets hard, don't look for excuses, and don't lose sight of your goal. Instead, tap into your own Samurai spirit.

Be True to Your Dreams (Don't Sell Out!)

When I delivered the rough cut of the 1996 *Eco-Challenge* show to Discovery Channel, they were unhappy. My creative team of Mike Sears, Tom Shelley, and Jay Bienstock (Tom and Jay still work with me today on *Survivor*) had raced against an incredible deadline. They were expected to produce a show in half the time we currently use. And they did. Not only was it the first time in TV history that an adventure race was to appear on television as a five-hour mini-series, but those guys managed to whittle several hundred hours of race footage into an action-packed television adventure in just ten short weeks.

Discovery had asked for a show with no narrator, and we did it. We felt it didn't work, but we agreed and were ready to add narration and change the show if Discovery allowed us. They panicked, however, and with only five weeks before the airdate. They gave our finished show to another production company with orders to make changes to hours one, two, and five. We were horrified. The changes were no different from what we'd proposed, yet we weren't being entrusted with our own program. When we later submitted the show for Emmy consideration, I chose to send hour number four, because it was one of those that was entirely finished by us. When we received word of the nomination we were ecstatic because we knew it was for our work, not the other production company's.

A rift began developing between Discovery and me. They envisioned *Eco-Challenge* as a pure documentary show focusing on nature—trees, animals, glaciers—with the athletes and race as secondary elements. I disagreed very strongly. *Eco-Challenge* was not a documentary, but a reality drama about men and women in harrowing, tortuous personal circumstances. The animals and nature were bit players in the race's larger drama.

Unfortunately, Discovery had total creative control of what aired on their network. Though I controlled the actual production, it was their vision of *Eco-Challenge* making its way onto television. I realized there was no way I could win. At Discovery's urging, I signed over control of *Eco-Challenge*'s television production in 1997. It was a three-year deal, giving Discovery exclusive rights until the summer of 1999. I would remain as executive producer, but the actual control was Discovery's. They decided to use another production company to shoot the race.

Discovery, however, soothed my anguish by doubling my salary. I figured it was a pretty good deal to get double the money for half the work. So, I swallowed my pride and took the money.

Despite working shoulder to shoulder with Discovery Channel's most experienced executive producer, Angus Yates, who had also become one of my closest friends, the first production under the new arrangement was hard. Discovery's accounting and production management departments split the budget into two business units, a television production and a race production. Angus and I agreed that was insane and far more expensive, but the issue was out of our control. I was in charge of the race budget, and could only chafe at the money wasted separating race and TV budgets. My dream was being absorbed by a corporate entity and I was in the awful position of standing there and watching it. Just two short years after Utah, when I'd had the courage to tell a major company that I wouldn't take their money, I was only too happy to sell out to Discovery. One could argue that I was being paid quite a bit more money, but the money mattered less and less. I believed that the point of *Eco-Challenge* was human drama, not a factual natural history documentary with a bit of people thrown in for color. Discovery's point of view was wrong, and violated every tenet of my Eco-Challenge dream. Nevertheless, they were in charge. It was an awful feeling.

The 1998 race in Morocco was substantially better. Angus had gained more control and as a result had brought in a new supervising producer, Paul Sparrow. We all got along great and he agreed it should be a drama about human relationships. We worked well together in the creative process. That was gratifying, because it was my fourth Eco-Challenge and I saw it in my head before we even started shooting. My creative muscles were growing. Honestly, it all goes back to what I said about trusting your gut. I had developed a very keen intuition for what works and doesn't work on television. For instance, when I envisioned the start in Morocco, I had a crystal-clear image of competitors atop camels, sprinting across that hard desert sand like a vision from *Lawrence of Arabia*. And that's how I started the race. It worked brilliantly. Through hours watching rough cuts of shows and collectively deciding what to keep in, what to keep out, and what elements needed to be added, I learned how great television should be structured. Combining that knowledge with my gut instinct fueled the growth of my creative ability.

The Morocco show was incredible. Thanks to Angus and Paul, I won my first Emmy. My ego was soothed, and I fooled myself into thinking that qualms about Discovery's control over Eco didn't bother me. In fact, when Greg Moyer, the man who'd brought Eco to Discovery as his pet project, made me an offer in 1998 that would provide for my family for many years to come, I agreed to the deal. Discovery would own *Eco-Challenge* outright—television rights, race production, everything.

Then just as we were about to sign the deal, Greg Moyer abruptly resigned from Discovery. In the confusion that followed at Discovery's corporate headquarters, the offer to purchase Eco was taken off the table.

I was panicked. I had stopped everything due to the anticipated deal and now, without it, my race may die.

However, just months later, in the spring of 1999, Discovery came to me with an alternate offer: They didn't want to buy the race but they still wanted to produce it. They would cut my fee in half, cut the race's budget in half, and then have me solicit corporate sponsorship dollars to make up the difference. Their argument was that they'd spent 40 million dollars on *Eco-Challenge* between 1996 and 1998, beaming the television show into those 145 million households in 140 countries. Despite the fact that they'd earned a handsome financial profit on their investment, Discovery

Now, that particular beach was known as Four-Mile Beach because it was exactly four miles long. At either end was a pile of jagged rocks and a sudden cliff, enclosing the beach. The photo shoot was to take place at roughly the midpoint of Four-Mile. So my horse had roughly two miles to gallop before smashing me headlong into the cliffs.

After a mile, a Rottweiler appeared from nowhere. The brutish beast squared off 200 yards in front of myself and the horse, barking ferociously. As if that wasn't bad enough, I now realized that my foot had slipped through the stirrups. If I slipped from the saddle I would get dragged along the beach, with a vicious dog nipping at my head as it bounced atop the sand. Luckily, the galloping horse was too much for the huge dog. As we thundered toward it, the dog whimpered and ran off.

I could see the end of the beach approaching, and that rock wall rising so hard and cold. Clearly, I had to make a decision, and had just seconds to do so.

I chose to steer the horse into the ocean. If I couldn't stop it on land, at least I could slow it down in the water. Then maybe I could untangle my foot and jump off. Of course, if I couldn't untangle my foot, and fell off anyway, I would drown. Given the choice between smashing headlong into a cliff or doing battle with the waves, I chose the waves.

Good decision.

I yanked hard on the left rein, trying to steer the horse into the water. Ever so slightly, it veered into the breakers and slowed down. That was just enough for the 14-year-old son of one of the wranglers, who, unknown to me, had given chase from the beginning upon seeing that I was out of control, to overtake us. He guided his horse alongside mine, reached across, grabbed the reins, and stopped my horse. "Little out of control there, mate," he said with that Australian gift for understatement.

Of course, we still had a photo shoot to accomplish, so not only did I have to ride my horse all the way back up the beach, but I had to ride that same horse for the next three hours in and out of the waves with the cameras rolling!! I was scared to death the whole time.

Looking back, it was a poor decision for me to underestimate my horse and overestimate my riding abilities. The ensuing adventure was the type I can do without.

The decision to guide my horse into the waves was a good one, though. It may have saved my life.

One bad decision. One good decision. However, for success to happen, decisions to act must be made. For those afraid of making decisions, fearful the sky will fall on them or they'll lose their job or whatever other reason a person can give for not taking control of their life, remember that by passively choosing not to decide, you've still made a choice. Better to make an empowering action-oriented decision than to decide to passively let life control you.

So be right or be wrong, but make a decision.

Go with Your Gut

I've written a great deal about going with your gut when it comes to making decisions. It's a process that cannot be underestimated for its power and prescience, and I think each of us knows that if we learn to trust that little voice showing the way to go, most decisions will turn out to be good ones. I'd even go so far as to say *all* decisions turn out for the best if you trust your gut.

Gut decisions, or intuition, are a combination of structured knowledge (acquired through books, formal education, and the like), life lessons (the continuum of successes and failures we've mentally catalogued since birth), and the vagaries of the decision-making scenario. When confronted with a situation requiring a decision, I think most of us would be surprised to know (at least, I believe this to be true) that the mind has already run through its database, appraised the situation, and made a decision. Sometimes the decision seems proper, sometimes it seems illogical. Either way, a decision has been made. That's the gut decision. That's the one to go with.

However, human nature tends to ignore the subconscious. We tend to laboriously analyze a situation, adding personal emotion (mood, relationships, fatigue, etc.) to the process. The decision, so crystal clear to the subconscious, becomes clouded. Very often, the wrong decision is made.

Again, this is all my own take on what comprises a gut

decision. I've never seen any scientific study defining the phenomenon, and I know many people either choose to deny the existence of intuition or ignore it altogether, but I can't emphasize its power firmly enough.

The challenges and adventures of Eco-Challenge had taught me to rely on my gut, but it was *Survivor* that made me put that skill to use each and every day. It was literally one tough decision after another. And you know, I can honestly say that very few were wrong. For instance, when it came time to select a host, I watched over a hundred audition tapes. But the minute I viewed Jeff Probst's, I knew he was perfect for *Survivor*. He wasn't famous, nor an expert adventurer, but my gut told me he was the one.

I also had a gut feeling all along that *Survivor* would be a hit. From the time Charlie Parsons and I first discussed my purchasing the rights at a 1996 Christmas party, to the day Les Moonves gave me the green light to begin production, I knew it would catch on with the American public. I felt this so strongly that when I pitched the show to Leslie Moonves at CBS, I began by handing him a mock cover of *Newsweek* with *Survivor* on the cover. I wanted him to know that I truly believed *Survivor* would be big. Why? Because my gut told me so. Who could resist watching sixteen strangers building a new world, then destroying it week by week, vote by vote? I believed the subject matter was universally interesting.

I put that philosophy to the test two months before production began, while I was still in Patagonia for Eco-

Challenge. The race was done and it was our last night before heading home. By then, a press release requesting *Survivor* applicants had made the front page of *USA Today*, yielding 6,000 homemade audition videotapes. My casting director, Lynn Spillman, had narrowed that initial bunch down to 800, then further whittled the field to 50 "gold star" finalists. All had the right stuff for the show. Lynn placed their videos on a single VHS tape for me to review, then FedExed it to Patagonia. Rather than watching the tape alone, in the vacuum of my hotel room, I invited the crew to come have beers in the alpine chalet by the finish line. Many were booked to work on *Survivor* eight weeks later, and I thought they might like to see what kind of men and women they would soon be seeing on a daily basis.

Secretly, however, I wanted their true reactions to the show. This was similar to those days when I practiced the *Survivor* pitch at dinner parties. I would play the video for the crew to get their reactions.

From the minute I popped that videotape in the chalet's VCR, the room quieted and everyone was captivated by those crazy tapes. The crew consisted of tough, outdoorsy, genuine people—and they couldn't get enough of *Survivor*. I knew those crew members well enough to know they would be honest with me, and if the potential *Survivor* cast was mediocre I would hear about it. But they watched, enthralled, as the would-be castaways creatively demonstrated why they should be on the island. There was the fireman who set his hat on fire, the woman who cooked her "steak" bikini, and a dance therapist who performed a dance routine for her audition. Sean Kenniff, who made the final cut, shot his video in the shower, surrounded by rubber snakes and spiders. Sonja Christopher played the ukelele and sang.

I was enthused that the crew loved the casting tapes so much, because I realized that the show—more than danger, more than survival, more than exotic location—was about people. It was a drama, and a drama is lost if it cannot hold its audience.

I flew home from Patagonia and began to focus entirely on *Survivor*. The question I was asked most often in the weeks and months leading up to production was "How will it begin?" People were buying into the dramatic pretext of the show, but I think they sensed that a great deal of its legitimacy hinged on how we actually got the castaways onto the island. The television audience needed to see these people being marooned. Having them dropped by helicopter or placed on the island by Zodiac inflatable boat shattered the illusion of being stranded. It was weak.

I'd thought of all that, and my gut immediately supplied the proper decision. "I'll have them jump off a boat with all their possessions," I'd tell whoever asked, "and the game will begin at that moment."

My gut told me that forcing the castaways to jump ship a mile offshore and swim to the beach would make a stunning visual and elicit a strong emotional response in viewers (who wouldn't be scared at the idea of literally leaping into the unknown?) that would make them want to watch more.

When I'd gone to Borneo in June of 1999 to scout locations, the helicopter had flown over a small fishing village. It was primitive and obviously indigenous, set in a small bay fronting the South China Sea. The houses were on stilts, with longboats and native fishing boats tied off on the stilts. It looked like something straight out of *Apocalypse Now,* and had the visual and cultural appearance that would immerse viewers in the exotic location immediately. I never told anyone at the time, but that village was where I was determined to shoot the opening moments of *Survivor.*

I had a visual inspiration, looking down on the village. Not only would the castaways leap from a boat into the water, but they would board the boat at this fishing village. This would say to the American public that, not only were the castaways about to be marooned on a forbidding jungle isle, but they would get there by leaving from a totally foreign, tiny, third-world fishing village.

However, when I returned to Borneo just prior to production, eight months later, the location scout didn't know what village I was talking about. He took me to a different village, one he felt was perfect for the opening. I took a look at the village he had in mind, but knew it wouldn't work. When I described the village I'd seen before, he looked at me like I was crazy. He said no such place existed. We flew up and down the coast for

144 DARE TO SUCCEED

hours one day, searching only for that village—and found no sign of it. I went back to my hotel room thinking he was right. I'd imagined the place.

I dug out the photographs I'd taken during that initial visit. There was a huge stack, and I examined each photo, searching for some sign of that elusive, perfect village. I despaired I would never find it, and *Survivor* would lose a vital bit of its essence and flavor. Yes, there were other fishing villages; Borneo's coast is pocked with them. But none were the one I wanted. I had always recognized the power of acting on visions; this village was ingrained in my brain. I was really unhappy that it possibly didn't exist at all.

Then I found a stack of photos I'd misplaced inside a zippered compartment on the side pocket of my luggage. There it was: the one and only picture I'd taken of that village. When I showed it to a few local chaps the next day, they told me exactly where my lost village could be found. My location scout and I flew there, and saw that it was as I remembered. Perfect. I had made the decision to shoot in that village, and stuck by it, even when told I was mistaken. Some might call that stubborn (it is), but belief in gut decisions means sticking to your guns, even when others say you're wrong.

The next step in making that opening scene perfect was finding the proper boat. We found the *Mata Hari* moored in the harbor in Kota Kinabalu, outside a luxury hotel. She was a native sailing ship, built by hand, without the use of nails. Her hull was yellow, with an orange image of the rising sun on her stern. Two masts. A bowsprit.

The owner was happy to participate in *Survivor's* filming, but she also let us know that *Mata Hari* was more suited to coastal cruising than open-ocean travel. She had made the 50-mile passage to Pulau Tiga once—barely. What's more, the journey took seven hours. This presented a pair of problems: first, safety. Would there be enough space on the camera boats to pull the castaways inside if *Mata Hari* sank? Second, cost. Filming every minute of a seven-hour trip would cost me a fortune. My dilemma was simple: Either I accepted the risks and financial obligations of filming on the *Mata Hari*, or my opening segment would have to be changed. But to what? I couldn't very well have 16 people leaping from the afterdeck of a fiberglass tri-hull. If I were going to do that, I might as well be filming an island version of *MTV's Beach House*.

I decided to take the risks. On the morning of March 13, 2000, *Survivor* production officially began. The call time was 4 A.M. The crew and I took speedboats out of Kota Kinabalu harbor to the fishing village of Sabang. It was pitch-black as we left the marina outside the Magellan. The boats had no running lights. Roaring into the predawn darkness was like entering one of those scary funhouse rides—I couldn't see what lay before me, but I knew the next 40 days and nights of *Survivor* production would be a thrill.

The castaways were also taken by speedboat in the

gray dawn from their hotel to Sabang. They looked disoriented, scared. They walked through the village in the early morning light, eyes wide, wary of the village, the cameras, each other. They donned orange life jackets and climbed into two colorful launches owned by the villagers. Then they motored out to *Mata Hari*, bobbing at anchor in the harbor. They sat like victims, knees drawn close, helpless. The sun was rising as they boarded *Mata Hari*, and their orange life jackets clashed with the hazy dawn and dark, smooth waters. They were still not allowed to speak to one another. I was struck by how normal they looked against the indigenous Sabang backdrop, and how unprepared they appeared for what was about to happen to them. "Weird to think," a crew member said as I stepped into a boat to board *Mata Hari*, "that soon all of America will be talking about them."

The cruise to Pulau Tiga went flawlessly. It was a seven-hour, "one take" day and we had a total of 23 cameras shooting almost continuously throughout the voyage, then flawlessly segued into shooting island reality once the castaways paddled ashore (a two-mile journey that took several hours in the equatorial sun. I felt extremely bad for the castaways, but happy that they surely knew *Survivor* wasn't a picnic.). I couldn't have asked for a better day. I knew as soon as I saw the rough-cut footage of Jeff Probst ordering the 16 very surprised castaways to take what they needed and leap from the *Mata Hari* that the show had a perfect beginning.